THE PRETRIBULATION RAPTURE THEORY AND DISPENSATIONALISM REVISITED

J. MIKE BYRD

WESTBOW
PRESS®
A DIVISION OF THOMAS NELSON
& ZONDERVAN

WestBow Press books may be ordered through booksellers or by contacting:

WestBow Press
A Division of Thomas Nelson & Zondervan
1663 Liberty Drive
Bloomington, IN 47403
www.westbowpress.com
1 (866) 928-1240

ISBN: 978-1-4908-3447-4 (sc)
ISBN: 978-1-4908-3448-1 (hc)
ISBN: 978-1-4908-3446-7 (e)

Library of Congress Control Number: 2014907403

Print information available on the last page.

WestBow Press rev. date: 10/19/2015

CONTENTS

List of Figures - vii

Preface - xi

CHAPTER 1 Methods of Interpretation - - - - - - - - - - - 1

CHAPTER 2 Dispensationalism and The
"Dispensational Principle" - - - - - - - - - - - - - 39

CHAPTER 3 "The Day of the Lord" - - - - - - - - - - - - - 65

CHAPTER 4 The "Imminence" Issue - - - - - - - - - - - - - 96

CHAPTER 5 The Rapture, the Resurrection
and the Second Coming of Christ - - - - - - 135

CHAPTER 6 Summary and Conclusions - - - - - - - - - 169

Bibliography - 175

LIST OF FIGURES

1.2.1 Interpretations and Theological
     Perspectives on Revelation   22

3.1.1-1 Day of The Lord   75

3.1.2-1 Comparison of Views – Day of Wrath   76

3.1.2-2 Comparison of Two Views: Pretribulation
        vs. Posttribulation Prewrath Rapture View   77

6.1 The Posttribulation Prewrath Rapture View   174

This book is dedicated to my own personal hero of the faith - my father, who lived a life of faith, faithfulness and obedience to the God whom I have come to know and trust largely because of him and his exemplary life.

PREFACE

Perhaps the most popular eschatological view of our day among conservative evangelical Christians is the Pretribulation Rapture view, which is associated with a school of Theology known as Dispensationalism. Proponents of the view are often dogmatic in their assertions that the Bible clearly teaches a rapture of the church immediately before a seven year "Tribulation Period," hence it is known as the "Pretribulation Rapture view." That seven-year "Tribulation Period" is consummated by a second coming of Christ to earth to judge the earth, and to set up a kingdom on earth in which He will reign absolute for 1000 years. They claim that their view is based on a strictly literal interpretation of Scripture, and is more literal than other competing eschatological views.

This view is one of many variations of what is broadly referred to as Futurism and Premillennialism, because they interpret much of prophetic Scripture, and in particular the Apocalypse, as related to events that have not yet occurred, that are still in the future. It is in contrast with what have been historically the more mainstream traditional views since as early as Augustine, that most of the "end-time" prophecy other than the ultimate return of Christ, has already been fulfilled, and/or is being fulfilled in this present age. This school, known generally as "Amillennialism" (meaning no literal Millennium) maintains that such apocalyptic passages as the book of Revelation and the Old Testament "ends-times" prophesies are meant to be interpreted figuratively as hyperbolic language typical of poetic apocalyptic literature. This falls into the broader category known as the historicist's school as opposed to futurists, and is similar to other schools including Preterism and Postmillennialism. These views are briefly addressed in the following work but the main focus is on the futurists' interpretations.

The purpose of this study is to attempt to evaluate objectively the various views primarily with respect to the controversial question of the Rapture of the Church, and related eschatological theories and interpretations of Scripture. While it is beyond the scope of this work to evaluate exhaustively all of the theories and views, or even all of the most prominent mainstream views, the more prominent futurists views are evaluated with respect to certain key issues and pivotal points of interpretation of Scripture. In paarticular the focus is primarily on the Pretribulation Rapture view, and the claims of proponents and adherents of that view. More recently a variation of the Futurists Premillennial Dispensationalists' view has emerged which is known as the Pre-Wrath Rapture view, which is also addressed.

As discussed in the following under Method of Interpretation, the approach taken in this study is to first determine as objectively as possible what the Word of God is saying, depending upon the Holy Spirit for enlightenment and guidance. This means that instead of looking to commentaries and the works of Theologians and other Bible scholars, the deliberate attempt is made to first become thoroughly familiar with all of the Scripture on the subject, and let Scripture interpret Scripture. That decade long exercise resulted in significant changes in my own beliefs and understanding with respect to end-times prophesy and related scenarios. It served as the foundation or basis for evaluation of the works of other men, some widely recognized as experts on the subject. It also involved critical thinking disciplines applying objective rules of interpretation (hermeneutics - emphasis on "objective"), and recognized rules of logic. The following is the product of an attempt to compare what such men have written, to what was gleaned from a personal first-hand in-depth study of the subject in Scripture.

The result of this study was not only to conclude that the prevalent theories evaluated all seem to have serious shortcomings with the possible exceptions of a few that are not so prevalent. More importantly the conclusion was reached that the shortcomings of these other views are resolvable by letting Scripture interpret Scripture, applying objective rules of interpretation, exegesis and logic. Hence a new scenario is proposed, which actually consists mostly of elements of existing theories, including some that are just beginning to emerge as current events unfold and prophetic details are being fulfilled.

The Key issues and pivotal points of interpretation of Scripture which are addressed in this work, will include the following:

- Methods of interpretation - allegorical, vs. hyperbolic and figurative vs. literal;
- "The day of the Lord" and "the Wrath of God," or "The day of the Lord's Wrath";
- The Destruction of the Present Heaven and Earth and the Creation of the New Heavens and Earth;
- The "imminence" issue - Preterists interpretation, vs. Pretribulation Rapturists doctrine, vs. scriptural teaching;
- The Rapture, Resurrection and Second Coming of Christ;

However, the question that is commonly being asked today is, what difference does it make? Does it really matter what we know or believe about end-times prophecy, and in particular the timing of the rapture? Ostensibly in the interest of avoiding divisions over such issues many Christians, including many pastors and teachers in our churches today are avoiding the subject altogether, or avoiding anything very definitive that would be meaningful but potentially divisive. Perhaps they are right, as long as you are living the Christian life like you should, it may not really matter. However, the following should be considered in accepting such an answer to such an important question.

First we see that a very significant portion of Scripture is devoted to this subject, including a whole rather major book, which closes out our Bibles. Much if not most of the Old Testament books of prophecy don't make a whole lot of sense, nor are they really relevant to us, if we adopt this attitude. Furthermore, while the desire for unity may be a genuine motivation, such an approach may also involve a lack of interest, an intellectual laziness, and a preference to remain ignorant to avoid the conflict that comes with standing for the truth. Unity that involves compromise with the truth of God's word is not the unity of the Spirit, not the kind of unity that Scripture encourages and exhorts us to pursue. And in this case, if we know and take seriously the exhortations and warning of Scripture, we see that knowing the truth about these matters will be critical for those living in the times being addressed in prophecy. And in fact, having the right attitude biblically speaking about these issues, may be more critical than many think with respect to whether or not they will indeed live their lives the way they should.

As we learn from the study of the book of Revelation, as well as related passages, there will be many who will be deceived by the spirit of the Antichrist, and the false teachers of every era, and in particular in those last days:

> *"For the time will come when they will not endure sound doctrine; but wanting to have their ears tickled, they will accumulate for themselves teachers in accordance to their own desires; and will turn away their ears from the truth, and will turn aside to myths." (2 Tim. 4:2)*

We see from Paul's letter to the Thessalonians that there will be many who will be deceived by "the lawless one" (Antichrist) because "they did not receive the love of the truth so as to be saved." As a result God Himself sends "a deluding influence so that they might believe what is false" (2 Thess. 2:8-12). It is significant here that the problem these people have is not just that they are deceived. The real problem is that they did not have "a love of the truth" - they didn't really want to know the truth. Thus God allows them to be deceived, and even sends a "deluding influence" such that no matter how obvious it becomes, or how apparent it should be that this world leader who offers global unity and worldwide peace, is actually Satanically empowered - they won't see it.

In fact, many professing believers may well believe it is God working all the mighty miracles through this great prophet (the "False Prophet"). They will be especially vulnerable to such a strong delusion if they believe in a Pre-tribulation Rapture, which would make them think that they won't even be here when the Antichrist arrives on the scene. The very fact that they are still here witnessing these events will be proof to them that it cannot be the Antichrist - since they are sure they will be raptured out before the Antichrist even appears. Not only atheists and non-believers but probably many "Christians" who do not now truly love the truth, will be deceived and will be co-opted by the global government system of the Beast. There will be many who will "fall away" from the faith (as per John 15:6; Heb. 6:6; 10:23-39; 2 Pet. 2:20-22). These are the ones Paul warned Timothy about in 2 Timothy 2:4 (cited above).

Certainly this is true of much of the Christian Church today, even among those who call themselves conservative evangelicals. Not only is the gospel they preach very watered down (easy believism, cheap grace, repeat the "sinner's prayer" and your "once saved always saved," come to Jesus to get what you want/need rather than as Lord, "death to self" no longer preached), but the popular doctrines accommodate fleshly tendencies to remain spiritually immature, weak in the faith, and virtually ignorant of God's Word. Christian's who believe that they were saved by praying a prayer, and can never lose that salvation no matter what, have little incentive to deny self, and endure temptation, trials, and even persecution - i.e. to take up their cross to follow Christ. People who believe that God is going to rapture them out before the time of testing and judgment begins on this earth, have little motivation to "be diligent to be found by Him in peace, spotless and blameless," careful to maintain "holy conduct and godliness, looking for and hastening the coming of the day of God because of which the heaven will be destroyed by burning and the elements will melt with intense heat" (2 Pet. 3:11-14). They prefer to believe in eschatological theories and scenarios that dogmatically insist on an escapist interpretation, denying the clear teaching of Peter that we should be motivated by the expectation of that day of God's judgment on earth. By distorting what Peter clearly articulated they insist that we don't even have to worry about that day as God will have us all out of here seven years before that day comes (and indeed many if not most aren't even interested in end-time prophecy).

For many it will be too late before they recognize the error of such teaching, but the root problem will be that they did not really love the truth - didn't really want to know the truth. Otherwise, God has clearly promised that anyone who wants to know the truth, enough to search for it, will find it (Matt. 7:7-8). This will not come, however, by reading men's books, or listening to the many explanations and declarations of men, but by looking to God, and depending upon Him to reveal it to them. It will come from searching His Word, and depending upon His Holy Spirit to guide and enlighten them in discerning what His Word is saying (John 14:16-17; 26; 17:17; 1 John 2:27).

Thus those who do not repent, even when they see the events and developments of the six trumpet judgments, will by that time be under the supernatural delusion sent by God. But they will have reached that point because they had no love for the truth, no real desire to know what God's Word is really saying. They will instead have bought into the false teachings and lies, which will eventually lead to being deceived by the worldwide system of the Beast and his miracle working False Prophet. How careful we need to be today to be sure that we are earnestly and sincerely seeking the truth, looking to God and His Word and depending upon His Holy Spirit within us to find that truth - not trusting in men, nor influenced by popular trends in the world or in the church of our day.

Hence the whole premise upon which this study is based is the belief that it definitely does matter what we believe about these subjects, including the timing of the rapture.

CHAPTER 1

METHODS OF INTERPRETATION

There are several factors that are the key players in determining how one will understand and interpret the Bible in general, and the prophetic passages in particular. Not surprisingly the most obvious is the **Method of Interpretation** to which one subscribes. Generally speaking there are those who interpret Scripture literally, and those who do not. Particularly with respect to prophecy, there are those who interpret Scripture allegorically - or mostly symbolically or figuratively - as opposed to those who interpret it more literally. The former argue that the literal, natural understanding of the text is not the intended message. This approach is applied to varying degrees throughout the Bible, to the extent that many who claim to be Christian would deny such essential doctrines as the deity of Christ, His virgin birth, His substitutionary death for our sin, and His supernatural bodily resurrection and ascension. Others believe that the very words in the original texts were inspired by God and therefore should be taken literally. However, even in the "literalists" camp there are disagreements with respect to the degree to which the written text should be interpreted literally. Some believe that the Bible is literal with regard to the essential teachings mentioned above, but find symbolic meaning behind literal statements of fact, the symbolism requiring interpretation and the meaning being spiritually instructive. For some the historical and most of the doctrinal passages and teachings of Scripture are to be taken as literally as possible, but the prophetic passages are not. To them the prophetic passages are written in hyperbolic or poetic language, which must all be taken figuratively and symbolically. Others claim to be literalists, but in the case of prophetic passages will often look for a symbolic meaning when such is neither necessary nor required by the text or context, and in fact a more literal meaning makes sense taken in its most natural, normal, and customary sense. Finally there is a small minority who consistently take even prophecy as literally as possible, while at the same time recognizing symbolism and figurative language when it is used or indicated by the text or the context.

With respect to the whole area of what is known as "Eschatology," dealing with what the Scripture reveals with respect to "end-times," or what we refer to as "prophecy," the method of interpretation is determinative with respect to the views ostensibly derived from them. As a result we have several major schools of thought on the subject, which are summarized in the following.

Idealism

The Idealists' approach to interpretation of Scripture is also known as Spiritualism, or the Symbolic approach. The typical definition of this view is that it interprets prophetic passages of Scripture symbolically as opposed to literally, and the message being conveyed is spiritual in nature. In general the intended message is concerning the struggle between good and evil, between light and darkness, and that the good and light ultimately wins out over evil and darkness. Apocalyptic passages are really only poetry, and do not have any significance with respect to past or future events, but are equally applicable to anyone in any age because of the spiritual nature of the message.

Preterism

Preterism (from the Latin *praeteritus,* meaning "gone by") is the school of interpretation that sees most, or all of prophecy as having already been fulfilled in the past. Preterists are divided between Partial, or Moderate Preterism, and Full, or Radical Preterism. R.C. Sproul gives the following definitions: "We may distinguish between the two distinct forms of preterism which I call radical preterism and moderate preterism. Radical preterism sees all future prophecies of the New Testament as having already taken place, while moderate preterism still looks to the future for crucial events to occur." (R.C. Sproul, <u>The Last Days According to Jesus</u>, p. 24). Full Peterism is more consistent in interpreting everything as having already happened, mostly in the first century AD. Preterists see most of Revelation as having been fulfilled in the Roman persecution of the early Christian church, and the destruction of Jerusalem in 70 AD.

Historicism

According to the Historicism Research Foundation the brief definition of "Historicism" is as follows:

"Historicism is unlike Preterism, which teaches that most of prophecy has been fulfilled in the past. It also differs from Futurism, which teaches that prophecy will only be fulfilled at some future date. In brief, Historicism teaches that biblical predictions are being fulfilled throughout history and continue to be fulfilled today. The Book of Revelation is a pre-written history of the Church from the time of its writing to the future Second Advent of Christ, which shall usher in the new heaven and new earth." ("What is Historicism," Historicism Research Foundation, www. historicism.net.)

Historicists have demonstrated a tendency to interpret prophecy and Revelation in particular, as finding fulfillment in the events and characters of their own time. This has resulted in many different interpretations down through the centuries. For example, according to the article cited above, "all historicists believe that the papacy is that man of sin of 2 Thessalonians 2, and a beast of Revelation 13."

Futurism

Futurism is the school of interpretation that interprets most eschatological prophecies as having future fulfillment. One of the most well known advocates of futurism, the late Dr. John Walvoord, gives the following brief definition in his introduction to his commentary on the book of Revelation: "...this point of view regards Revelation as futuristic beginning with chapter 4 and therefore subject to future fulfillment ... Under this system of interpretation, the events of chapter 4 through 19 relate to the period just preceding the second coming of Christ. This is generally regarded as a period of seven years with emphasis on the last three and one-half years, labeled the 'great tribulation.' Chapter 19, therefore, refers to the second coming of Christ to earth, chapter 20 to the future millennial kingdom which will follow, and chapters 21 and 22 to events either contemporary or subsequent to the millennium." (John Walvoord, The Revelation of Jesus Christ, pp. 20-21)

With the exception of the school known as "Futurism," the method of interpretation of Scripture involves varying degrees of the allegorical or symbolic method of interpretation. When it comes to this book of Revelation, such allegorical approaches leave it virtually wide open to any kind of speculation and imaginative interpretations which the reader chooses to ascribe to any given object or events found in the book. Some of course apply more discipline than others in relating their interpretations to other teachings in Scripture. However, while the possible range of varying and even conflicting interpretations using such approaches lead to many interesting scenarios, and philosophical theories, the end result is many differences of opinion and hence much confusion, but nothing of substance that can be objectively evaluated.

There is an old adage to the effect that something which means everything and anything, means nothing. Most allegorical approaches to interpreting the Bible, including the book of Revelation, may appeal to people in that they can be used to interpret the book in almost any way one wants to interpret it, limited and guided only by one's theological presuppositions. In these post-modern times when it is unfashionable and politically incorrect to believe in absolutes - that there is absolute reality and absolute truth - this is quite acceptable as long as no one claims that their interpretation is any better or more correct than anyone else's. The absurdity and futility of such foolhardy nonsense should be self-evident. Furthermore, it hardly seems worth one's time and effort to invest much in studying or trying to understand a book that has no real objectively identifiable meaning - especially if it is perceived as being prophetic in nature.

There is the other approach to interpreting Scripture, and even Revelation - **the literal approach**. Obviously this is not to suggest that there is no symbolism in the Bible, or in Revelation, because that also would clearly be absurd. Many if not most significant literary works incorporate a certain amount of symbolism. Throughout the Bible we find metaphors, analogies, anthropomorphisms, similes and idioms used to communicate a message. We find symbols used from the opening chapters of Genesis to the last chapter of Revelation (the "tree of life" for example). However, we also find literal text that explains what the intended meaning and message is. God has not left it up to our imagination, or even our creativity in using Scripture, to discern what He is trying to communicate. Adequate and consistent explanations for the symbolism in Scripture are provided in the literal text, as taken naturally without the need for human manipulations.

In a prophetic book like Revelation, or Daniel, there is more reliance on the use of symbolism, and in many cases the literal explanation is not readily obvious. As is always the case, a certain amount of discipline is required in the interpretation of the symbols, such as rules of logic and realistic and rational thinking. Logical and rational thinking is not to be confused with humanistic naturalism, and cannot exclude or preclude the supernatural, especially if we are to make any sense at all out of this book. But neither does the presence of involved symbolism, nor the acceptance of the supernatural, in any way excuse the lack of discipline in one's thought processes. **To accept the supernatural is not the same as accepting circular reasoning, or non-sequiturs, or inconsistent or self-contradictory statements or conclusions, or subscribing to two or more propositions that are mutually exclusive by their very nature.** For an interpretation to be valid it must be consistent with all of the known facts, cannot be simply ad hoc, or based on presuppositions which themselves are arguable and unproven.

In the case of Scripture, if we truly believe that it is God who has communicated to us through human agents (in this case John), then we have a valuable, indeed indispensable source of information about what is absolutely true and real. Symbols and symbolic language are either explicitly and quite adequately explained in literally articulated Scripture, or can be inferred from such Scripture. The "tree of life," for example, is clearly the symbol of the eternal life, the life of God that is from God - the spiritual life that is in and of the Spirit of God. It is not hard to figure out that there is probably not an actual physical tree somewhere over in the East or Middle East, with an angel standing guard to keep people away. Nor will there be such a physical tree in heaven, from which everybody in heaven will pick fruit to ingest and digest physically. [1] Nevertheless, the fact is that it is a symbol being used, and its' intended meaning is fairly clear from Scripture.

Of course, when it comes to a woman riding on the back of a beast with ten horns and ten crowns, the interpretation is not so obvious. However, in light of the literal explanations in the text (Rev. 13 & 17-18) and other related prophecies (such as found in the book of Daniel) and passages of Scripture, the intended meaning becomes more apparent. As history unfolds and these prophecies are fulfilled the specific meaning also becomes more apparent - and will become more apparent probably just at the time when they are more relevant to the readers.

In the case of Scripture however, we have the added responsibility of determining what the text, or texts, actually say. Here it becomes essential that the best available approach to exegesis be applied. Perhaps as much as scholarship this requires a high degree of intellectual integrity, as the temptation to translate a word or a passage to fit one's presuppositions seems almost irresistible to most men. [2] The literal approach is very sensitive to, and dependent upon such accurate and objective exegesis.

The approach taken in this study is to take the text as literally as possible within the constraints of what is logically feasible, allowing for the supernatural where such is indicated in the text. [3] Particular attention is given to accurate exegesis, and consistency with respect to other passages of Scripture, based on the premise that God's Word provides the best commentary on God's Word. The attempt is made to abandon and discard presuppositions, in order to let the author's intended message emerge from the text itself, including the doctrines and the scenarios derived from it.

---

1 It may be that there will actually be a physical tree in God's earthly eternal kingdom which provides sustenance and health, as portrayed in Ezekiel 47:12, but the tree in Revelation is very likely intended to be symbolic.

2 A case in point would be the debate that goes on over the little preposition "ek" in Rev. 3:10 - "I will keep you from [ek] the hour of testing…". It is hard to believe the abuses of exegetical techniques employed by men of considerable reputation in the evangelical community to make this verse support a view driven by certain doctrinal presuppositions.

3 For example, a mountain is taken as a mountain and a star is taken as a heavenly body, unless the text indicates other wise, as in Revelation 12:1 & 4 and 17:9-10, respectively.

1.1 Literal versus Allegorical Interpretation (Futurists vs. Preterists)

With respect to the reliability, reality, and relevance of the various interpretations of prophecy the issue of method of interpretation becomes a very critical subject that has long been the topic of much debate. However, one would have to question the wisdom of those who claim to believe that it is the Word of God, but then choose to believe that it is entirely allegorical, full of hyperbole and poetic language, so that the scenes and events which are described are hardly recognizable in their fulfillment. In this category would be those who are known as Historicists and Preterists (of various stripes), who would have us believe that all or most of what we see in the book of Revelation has already been fulfilled. Ironically such men claim an advantage with respect to credibility as they point to what appear to be weaknesses in the futurist's position, even attacking the Dispensationalists on the grounds of failures to interpret Scripture literally enough. The irony of this is that the Preterist's position is premised upon the denial that either Old Testament or New Testament prophecy should be interpreted literally or understood naturally. Rather they insist that they must all be seen as allegorical or "hyperbolic" - a euphemism for "grossly exaggerated." Selectively they choose to interpret a few passages more literally - so they claim - than do the Dispensationalists and Futurist (such as Matthew 24:34). However they ignore the fact that their interpretations of such passages are debatable at best, and may beg the question more than answer it.

Among those who believe that Scripture is to be interpreted allegorically, the most consistent are those who reject what the Bible tells us about the historic Jesus (including His virgin birth, miracles He performed, and His resurrection) and the essential doctrines of our faith (the depravity of man, the Hypostatic union of human and divine in Christ, the substitutionary atoning death of Christ, the realities of heaven or hell, etc.). These we know as liberal theologians, who make up their own versions of Christianity, and depend upon their own intellect (and imagination) and that of their peers who agree with them. What is wrong with this picture?

Then there are those who seem to have no problem with being inconsistent in their method of interpretation of Scripture. While insisting that certain parts and passages of the Bible must be taken literally, such as history and doctrine (exclusive of doctrines related to Eschatology), the prophetic parts are not to be taken literally. Prophetic passages, they insist, are in the same category as the poetry of Psalms, Proverbs, Ecclesiastes and Song of Solomon (which of course even the futurists and Dispensationalists recognize as full of allegory). This might not be a problem logically speaking except for two related problems. First, even when it comes to the interpretation of prophecy these men are inconsistent. To cite just one example, while telling us that the book of Daniel is prophetic, and hence according to their view should be taken allegorically instead of literally, they nonetheless point to and acknowledge historic events which actually fulfilled a literal interpretation of part of what Daniel prophesied. Like the futurists, they acknowledge that historic figures such as King Nebuchadnezzar and Alexander the Great (the "shaggy goat" Dan. 8:21) and Antiochus Epiphanes IV (Dan. 8:9-12 & 11:31) fulfilled Daniel's prophesies in the eighth chapter, and this requires a literal interpretation allowing of course for the symbology being used (as both camps do). However, when Daniel says that he is prophesying about the "end time," and the "last days," this they say should not be taken literally. When there is no corollary in the historic record to what Daniel prophesies, they have to resort to non-literal interpretations to force them to match historic events, since they have pre-supposed that Daniel's reference to "latter days" and "end time" cannot be still future. When Daniel prophesies about "a time, times, and half a time," saying that the "little horn" [4] will "devour the whole earth and tread and crush it" (Dan. 7:23), we are told it is hyperbolic language - it can't be taken literally. When we are told by Daniel that the demise of this world ruler will mark the beginning of a time when "the sovereignty, the dominion, and the greatness of all the kingdoms under the whole heavens and earth will be given to the people of the saints of the Highest One," a kingdom which will be "an everlasting kingdom" in which "all dominions will serve and obey Him" (Dan. 7:27) - we are told that this day has already come and we are now already living in it. What's more, according to their view, we are currently ushering in this everlasting kingdom (who would have guessed it).

To many of us such interpretations sound like utter nonsense on the face of it. To accept such explanations we either have to believe that Daniel's

---

4 The "little horn" is one of the "ten horns" on the head of the fourth Beast of Daniel 7 which clearly corresponds to the ten horned beast of Revelation 12, 13 and 17.

words have no absolute, recognizable meaning or we have to conclude that his prophesies were at best very misleading - gross exaggerations of reality. Some theologians may be able to convince themselves that we are living in such a promised age, but it will never fly with critical thinkers who insist on dealing with reality. There is no sense in which even today's Christians, the church, are reigning now over "the sovereignty and dominion and greatness of all the kingdoms under the whole heaven" (Daniel 7:27), let alone the nation Israel to whom this prophecy was first given. In fact not even a small portion of anything on earth is under the dominion of "the saints of the Highest One" anymore than any other time since the creation. There is no sense in which "all dominions" are serving and obeying Him - at least as far as this observer can discern - except in the sense that God is and always has been sovereign.

Perhaps even more ironic is the fact that the closer the Preterists get to the clear teaching of Scripture, the more inconsistent their approach to interpreting prophecy. Many if not most Preterists have had to acknowledge that there is a future coming of Christ to earth to once and for all judge the earth, and set up that eternal kingdom prophesied by Daniel. In the words of R.C. Sproul:

> "Radical preterism sees all future prophecies of the New Testament as having already taken place, while moderate preterism still looks to the future for crucial events to occur." [5]

Thus they selectively take certain New Testament passages, and even some in Revelation, as being quite literal. Their criteria for determining which passages are to be taken literally, and which should be relegated to allegorical hyperbolic language seem to be somewhat arbitrary, lacking in objectivity. Such determinations seem to be made based on their presuppositions - a dangerous approach when left in the hands of such finite humans. The "moderate" or "partial Preterists" cannot even appeal to the hermeneutic that all prophecy is in allegorical language, hyperbolic and poetic in nature - hence it's up to their own wisdom to discern what is or what isn't literal. The result is that some men would apparently see the resurrection of Revelation 11:18 and 20:1-6 as a literally future event, but

---

5 Sproul, R.C., <u>The Last Days According to Jesus</u>, Introduction, "Moderate Preterism", Baker Books, 1998 (fourth printing June 2003), p.24.

the establishment of Christ's millennial reign on this earth as something which has to be taken allegorically (though Sproul himself does not seem to be taking a position on this in the book cited above). [6]

Perhaps the main distinction between the "moderate Preterists" and "futurists," or "Premillennialists," would be their respective interpretations of the Olivet Discourse in Matthew 24. The former (and in particular Sproul) maintain that Jesus' prophecy in Matthew was fulfilled "in substance" in AD 70 as was the bulk of Revelation. This they argue despite the fact that Matthew's prophecy clearly parallels the developments we find in Revelation, and both are clearly referring to the "day of the Lord" return of Christ. The latter (Premillennialists) see this rather apparent correspondence, and recognize the seemingly obvious fact that neither the events prophesied in Matthew 24, nor the corresponding events of Revelation, have been fulfilled by any known historic events, unless we water them down to virtual meaninglessness [7] - which the allegorical approach allows us to do. Hence the partial or moderate Preterists come under attack from both sides, the full or "Radical" Preterists as well as the futurists for the same glaring discrepancy - inconsistency in their approach to interpretation.

Of course the Preterists of both stripes do have some legitimate criticisms of most futurists positions, in particular the widely popular Pretribulation Rapture position. While men like Walvoord and Pentecost are certainly more consistently literal in their approach to interpreting

---

6 Sproul is not clear on his position on this in his book, <u>The Last Days According to Jesus,</u> but does admit to identifying with the partial Preterists position of men such as Ken Gentry (p. 158). He also identifies with the Reformed theology school about which he makes the admission that "the majority report among Reformed thinkers tend to be amillennialism" (p. 195). However, in fairness he also states: "To be completely candid, I must confess that I am still unsettled on some crucial matters." (p. 158).

7 The dramatic cataclysmic events of the sun and moon and heavens and the sign of the Son of Man appearing of Matthew 24:27-31, which clearly corresponds to the prophecy by John in Revelation 1:7, and the sixth Seal events of Revelation 6:12-17, and the seventh Trumpet events of Revelation 11:15-19, and the seventh Bowl of Revelation 16:17-20, and the day of the Lord events of Revelation 19, don't come close to matching anything that has occurred in the known history of mankind. Nor does the destruction of tiny Jerusalem seem to fulfill the prophecies about the destruction of the heavens and earth and all its inhabitants as per Zephaniah 1 and 2 Peter 3:9-18.

Scripture than are the Preterists and Amillennialists, they are often guilty of ignoring some obvious facts literally articulated in Scripture, and introducing meanings to texts that simply aren't in those texts nor derivable from them, if they were using accepted methods of exegesis and intellectually honest approaches to hermeneutics. These inconsistencies in their approaches give the Preterists and others a lot of ammunition to support their contentions that the futurists are not consistently literal either. For example, taken literally there is nothing in Scripture which states or even implies that there will be a rapture of the church seven years before Christ's coming to earth - this is a product of Dispensational presuppositions.

Again, it is however ironic that the Preterists (including Partial Preterists) claim the high ground with respect to literal interpretation of Scripture. In fact the most convincing element of their argument, and perhaps the crux of the issue with respect to their criticisms against futurists, is centered around the interpretation of one word in Matthew 24:

> *"Truly I say to you, this* **generation** *will not pass away until all these things take place." (Matthew 24:34)*

Indeed, when we read this verse and we understand the word "generation" in the sense that it is used today in English, we would have to say that the futurists are in trouble, at least with respect to Matthew 24 (and by logical extension, all the corresponding passages mentioned above in Revelation). This combined with a number of passages which seem to be indicating that Christ's return would be imminent, that He would be coming back soon, they believe allows them to make the claim that they are the ones who are interpreting Scripture more literally. One of those passages that seems to be indicating imminence appears in the epilogue to the book of Revelation (Rev. 22:7, 12, & 20): "Behold I am coming quickly" (discussed in the following commentary). This, taken together with the Preterist's interpretation of Matthew 24:34 (cited above) would seem to support their argument that Jesus must have already come or else He hasn't really kept His word, since these promises were made over 1900 years ago. The critical question is whether that is what Jesus meant - is it the best interpretation of those passages?

1.1.1 "This Generation" (Matthew 24:34)

With respect to the heart of the Preterist's argument, Matthew 24:34, David Chilton, makes the following arguments:

> "This means that *everything* Jesus spoke of in this passage, at least up to verse 34, *took place before the generation then living passed away.* 'Wait a minute,' you say. 'Everything? The witnessing to all nations, the Tribulation, the coming of Christ on the cross, the stars falling ... *everything?*' Yes - and incidentally, this point is a very good test of your commitment to the principle we began with in this chapter. *Scripture interprets Scripture*, I said; ... Some have sought to get around the force of this text by saying that the word *generation* here really means *race*, and that Jesus was simply saying that the Jewish race would not die until all these things took place. Is that true? I challenge you: Get out your concordance and look up every New Testament occurrence of the word *generation* (in Greek, *genea*) and see if it ever means 'race' in any other context." (David Chilton, The Great Tribulation, Chapter 1, "This Generation.") [8]

Certainly Chilton seems to be making a valid point here. And certainly we can't fault his recommended approach. It is especially important for literalists to let Scripture interpret Scripture. So it does make sense to do as he recommends. But, if we do so, will we necessarily reach the same conclusions, without sharing first his presuppositions and biases in interpreting those other passages where this word is used?

If we go to the first passage where the Greek word appears, Matthew 1:17, it would appear as though Chilton is right. Matthew was pretty clearly referring to generations of people - not a race of people. Perhaps the argument could be made that a few of the other passages use this word similarly, to refer specifically to a group of people living in the same age or time frame. However, according to Greek scholars (Lexicographers) this

---

8 Chilton, David, The Great Tribulation, Dominion Press, 1987, pp. 2-3. It is interesting that Mr. Chilton chose not to mention the phenomenon of the sun being darkened, the moon not giving its light, as well as the stars falling (Matt. 24:29) when he boldly asserts that all these prophecies have already been fulfilled, and in fact were fulfilled by 70AD.

is not a meaning that is inherent in the Greek word itself. Joseph Henry Thayer gives four variations of the meaning of this word:

> 1. a beginning, birth, nativity; ... 2. passively, that which has been begotten, men of the same stock, a family; ... a. prop. ... the several ranks of men in a natural descent, the successive members of a genealogy: ... b. metaph. a race of men very like each other in endowments, pursuits, character; and esp. in a bad sense a perverse race: ... 3. the whole multitude of men living at the same time : ... 4. an age ..."

A very similar set of interpretations of this Greek word is provided by Arndt and Gingrich in the Walter Bauer Lexicon, <u>A Greek Lexicon of the New Testament and Other Early Christian Literature</u>. Apparently Chilton is convinced that the word has only one narrow meaning, the one necessary to make his case. But in fact recognized Greek scholars inform us otherwise. The root word itself seems to simply refer to a group of people that have something in common, which could be race, or family, or all living in the same age or time frame. Only the context tells us which of these is intended if it is anything beyond a simple reference to a group of people that is in some way related.

With this in mind, as we look at most of the references cited by Chilton, or found in our concordance (such as <u>The Englishman's Greek Concordance of the New Testament</u> by G.V. Wigram) we find that in fact most passages where this word is used are **not necessarily referring to groups of people living at the same time in that time is not the issue**. While translators have chosen the English word "generation", in most cases nothing in the context requires anything more than the word "people," or "people group." Sometimes it is referring to the Jews as a people group as is the case in most of the appearances of the word in the Gospels. In Luke 1:48 it refers to all people, or all people groups - all those generated on the earth. In Philippians 2:15 we see it used as follows:

> *"that you may prove yourselves to be blameless and innocent, children of God above reproach in the midst of a crooked and perverse **generation**, among whom you appear as lights in the world," (Philippians 2:15)*

Here in Philippians we see it used in a more general sense, not referring to a nation or race, or necessarily a group of people only living at the same time, but rather referring to a group of people who share the characteristics of being crooked and perverse. Because we understand it this way we know that it has equal application to us today even though we are not part of that "generation" living at the time Paul penned the words.

Thus, for Chilton to argue that he is right because he is letting Scripture interpret Scripture is to commit the same error that those against whom he is arguing also commit. Dispensationalists also insist that they are letting Scripture interpret Scripture when they cite passages such as Revelation 3:10 to support their interpretation of 2 Thessalonians 2:7, or vice versa. By forcing an unnecessary translation of certain words on the one text (such as the Greek word "ek" in Rev. 3:10) one finds substantiation for a forced interpretation of the other text (the "church" being the "restrainer" which is "taken out of the way" in 2 Thess. 2:7). Similarly, by insisting that every time the Greek word *"genea"* is used it always refers to only one out of four or five possible translations of the word regardless of context, is to be intellectually dishonest (albeit probably not intentionally dishonest as he really believes what he is saying is true).

1.1.2. "Behold I am coming quickly" (Rev. 22:6-7)

"And he said to me, 'These words are faithful and true; and the Lord, the God of the spirits of the prophets, sent His angel to show to His bond-servants the things which must shortly take place. And behold, I am coming quickly. Blessed is he who heeds the words of the prophecy of this book'." (Revelation 22:6-7)

John again repeats a statement that appears in his introduction to this book in the first verse. Writing about this revelation that he has received from God he refers to it as "the things which must shortly take place." (Rev. 1:1) In our text in 22:7 he adds to that: "And behold, I am coming quickly."

This brings us back to our text. Is God using John to tell us that Jesus was promising to come back soon, as in a short period of <u>human</u>

time after His first appearance on this earth? Here again we have a Greek word, or words, which involve a certain degree of ambiguity when we try to translate it or interpret it. The words used in Revelation 22:6 and 7, and for that matter in 1:1 and 22:20, are *tacei* and *tacu*, which are both derived from *tacus*. According to Thayer's Lexicon this word should be translated "quick, fleet, speedy". Similarly according to Bauer's Lexicon (Arndt & Gingrich), "quick, swift, speedy", indicating that when it is used in the neuter singular adverbial form (as it is in our text in 22:7) the first rendering is "quickly, at a rapid rate" and secondly "without delay, quickly, at once." The last possible rendering that they mention is "in a short time, soon."

H.K. Moulton in The Analytical Greek Lexicon Revised (1978 edition) specifically mentions the form of the word as it appears in 22:6 (and in 1:1 and again in 22:20), *en tacei*, rendering it "with speed, quickly, speedily; soon, shortly ... hastily, immediately". Thus most of the renderings by the Greek scholars who are only trying to get to the meaning of the word itself, is that it communicates the suddenness of something, with a secondary meaning that it sometimes communicates the imminence or "soonness" of something relative to something else. Once again we have a word that has a basic root meaning, but is used in various ways and takes on different nuances of that meaning depending upon how it is used in the context. To insist that the Greek word used here can only mean imminence as opposed to suddenness or the speed with which something prophesied will actually happen, is to simply show one's bias. Unless something in the context requires it the latter interpretation should be preferred to the former.

Of course when we look at the context of both of these passages, chapter one and chapter twenty-two, we do find other passages that seem to suggest that imminence or temporal proximity may be intended:

*"And he said to me, 'Do not seal up the words of the prophecy of this book, for **the time is near.**'" (Revelation 1:3)*

*"Blessed is he who reads and those who hear the words of the prophecy, and heed the things which are written in it; for **the time is near**." (Revelation 22:10)*

Here we do have a word that primarily indicates proximity, or nearness. It can refer to proximity in space or in time. It is often translated "at hand" in the King James Version. Since in the context here in Revelation the subject is future events that are going to happen, it probably makes little sense to say that spatial proximity is intended. Rather it seems logical that the intended meaning is that what is prophesied in this book is not that far away temporally speaking. Hence, the Preterit's say that their interpretation is more literal when they insist that it has all already been fulfilled in AD 70.

One problem with this argument is that most scholarship tends to favor a later date than AD 70 for the writing of these prophecies. Although scholars who hold to the Preterist's view of course question this, the evidence for a later date is somewhat compelling. According to one of the earliest and most recognized church historians Eusebius (AD 263-339), who twice quotes from an even earlier source, Irenaeus (2nd century Bishop of Lyon, student of Polycarp who was a disciple of the Apostle John) addressing this question of the date of the writing of the book:

> "For it was not seen a long time back, but almost in my own lifetime, at the end of Domitian's reign." (Irenaeus, Book III of Heresies Answered) 9

Since we know that Domitian's reign did not end until well after AD 70 (AD 96 according to historians), it would seem to be fairly conclusive that according to a reliable witness John did not write this book at some earlier date before AD 70. Certainly if John had written before that momentous date, and had been writing about the events fulfilled at that time, Irenaeus would have known that, and would have so indicated. Hence the burden of proof is on those who would now try to refute the testimony of witnesses so close to the time of all those events.

Another consideration is that we first see this expression used in Matthew, and Jesus said that after we see the cataclysmic sign events affecting the sun and moon and stars (also prophesied with more detail

---

9 Eusebius, The History of the Church from Christ to Constantine, Book 5, 8.9; Penguin Books, Dorset Press, 1965, p.211.

by Joel in Joel 2:28, which we see again in the sixth Seal of Rev. 6:12-17) then the time is near:

> *"even so you too, when you see all these things, recognize that He is near, right at the door." (Matt. 24:33)*

It is hard to believe that intelligent men would try to tell us that all of these prophesied events have already taken place any time in history, let alone in that singular event in AD 70. The events that they cite as fulfillment are almost laughable unless one subscribes to their method of interpretation of the words used, which is anything but literal in any sense of the word. However, if one does subscribe to such methods then it can certainly be argued that their interpretations are as good as anyone else's, and vice versa - we are completely at the mercy of men to reveal to us what God meant. This is a hermeneutic which this author rejects completely as antithetical to the whole concept of divine Revelation and the enlightenment ministry of the Holy Spirit.

Furthermore, keeping this use of the word "generation" in context of Matthew 24, we see that Jesus goes on in the very next verse (Matt. 24:35) to mention that "heaven and earth" will pass away, which would seem to be connected with these other events being prophesied. Surely no one should be taken too seriously who would suggest that this has already been fulfilled in any sense of the words used.

Once we understand that Matthew 24:34 could be just as correctly, and probably more accurately translated "this **people** shall not pass away until all these things take place" - indeed as it is most often used elsewhere, letting Scripture interpret Scripture - then the Preterists house of cards begins to crumble. Their only claim to being more literal than the futurists would appear itself to be an unsubstantiated claim. This supposed fatal blow to Dispensationalism, and futurist's claims to being more consistently biblical, is itself dealt a fatal blow, it would seem.

With respect to the allusions to the temporal proximity (nearness) or imminence of these events, and especially Christ's return, we see a very adequate explanation given by Peter:

> *"Know this first of all, that in the last days mockers will come with their mocking, following after their own lusts, and saying, 'Where is*

the promise of His coming? For ever since the fathers fell asleep, all continues just as it was from the beginning of creation.' For when they maintain this, it escapes their notice that by the word of God the heavens existed long ago and the earth was formed out of water and by water, through which the world at that time was destroyed, being flooded with water. But the present heavens and earth by His word are being reserved for fire, kept for the day of judgment and destruction of ungodly men.

But do not let this one fact escape your notice, beloved, that **with the Lord one day is as a thousand years, and a thousand years as one day***. The Lord is not slow about His promise, as some count slowness, but is patient toward you, not wishing for any to perish but for all to come to repentance. But the day of the Lord will come like a thief, in which the heavens will pass away with a roar and the elements will be destroyed with intense heat, and the earth and its works will be burned up. Since all these things are to be destroyed in this way, what sort of people ought you to be in holy conduct and godliness, looking for and hastening the coming of the day of God, on account of which the heavens will be destroyed by burning, and the elements will melt with intense heat! But according to His promise we are looking for new heavens and a new earth, in which righteousness dwells." (2 Pet. 3:3-12)*

Here Peter acknowledges that there will be a significant enough time delay between the time the promises of Christ's return and the time of their fulfillment – including the judgment of the whole heavens and earth - that men will mock the whole idea. Their mockery will be premised upon the fact that despite the ominous threats nothing has happened for a long time. If in fact these promises were fulfilled in AD 70 as the Preterists insist, then what Peter wrote here would make no sense at all, and would be at best completely unnecessary. Of course, if it was fulfilled in the relatively insignificant local event of the destruction of tiny Jerusalem, none of the prophecies are very meaningful or make much sense including Peter's words here in that they appear to describe a global event and beyond that to a cosmically apocalyptic event. To suggest that what Peter is describing here, which matches what Jesus and several of the Old Testament prophets described, was fulfilled in the Romans destroying one small city, is on the face of it, patently absurd. But to then claim the moral high ground on interpreting Scripture literally because of such an absurd obviously non-literal interpretation is almost unbelievably self-contradictory. [10]

Peter's explanation needs no further explanation. Scripture, and particularly prophecy is written from God's perspective when it comes to time, and the timing of events. With God, who is eternal, a thousand years is like a day. This means that though a few thousand years have elapsed, from God's perspective it's only like a couple of days. Thus when He promises that these events will take place soon, He may well mean within a few thousand years. This would be quite deceptive were it not for the fact that He has told us through Peter that this is what He means. If anyone denies that this is what Peter means by what he clearly writes, it may be quite telling to hear what his or her explanation of this passage would be.

It seems quite clear that God wanted the believers in that first century church to be looking for and expectantly awaiting Christ's return – they were repeatedly exhorted to do so. It also appears as though He has wanted believers of every age since then to be looking for His return, and as Peter wrote, to be living differently in light of our expectation that He is coming. Thus this element of imminence is what God intended when He gave us these promises. Even if we don't hold to the questionable teaching that Christ is coming before the time of Great Tribulation, and could have come any time since His departure from this earth, probably every generation has had reason to believe that the time was very near. Even if we do take 2 Thessalonians 2 quite literally without forced manipulations to spin the meaning, and we see that the "lawless one" (commonly referred to as the "Antichrist") will be revealed before Christ returns to gather us to Himself (2 Thess. 2:1-4), throughout history there have been what appeared to be Antichrists, and have been believed to be the Antichrist by many, beginning with Nero and Diocletian of

---

10 To suggest that it is "more literal" to take a few words like "generation" and "near" in their most narrow and unnecessarily restrictive sense, and then render virtually meaningless all the other descriptions of these end time events by dismissing them as hyperbolic language and symbolism, seems almost disingenuous, certainly inconsistent.

the early church era, through Hitler and Mussolini and more recently Khrushchev and even Saddam Hussein of our time. In the last 50 years of this observers existence the sense of the imminence of Christ's return has been prevalent and prominent amongst many true believers, and theories about the Beast and the Woman and who the Antichrist will be have not been in short supply.

God knew what He was doing when He inspired the writers of Scripture to portray this most momentous and climactic event as coming soon. He also was honest in explaining through Peter what He meant, and why He was portraying it this way.

Nonetheless, what all these views have in common is that they all recognize this as God's Word, divinely inspired, inerrant, accurate and reliable. And in fact much of the debate between the various factions are motivated by attempts to defend this premise, that God used John and Matthew and the other prophets and writers of Scripture to write these things, therefore they must all make sense and must all agree without contradictions. Unfortunately as men we all have severe limitations (this author being no exception), the biggest being our inability to recognize our own presuppositions and see the affects of our own biases on our reasoning processes. Intellectual honesty is not naturally adhered to by anyone, especially once one has become convinced they know the answers. It is the most natural human tendency to take a certain amount of evidence and draw conclusions, and then try to make the rest of the evidence fit those conclusions. This is probably why very well intended men, with high degrees of scholarship and sometimes impressive credentials, looking at the same set of evidence, will come to quite different conclusions.

However, to suggest that all such conclusions are going to be equally valid (a Christianized version of relativistic thinking), is of course absurd and obviates the need for anyone even trying to draw any conclusions. There are objective rules, if you will, that must be followed guiding our reasoning (Logic), and our interpretation of any literature, especially Scripture (Hermeneutics, Exegesis). To the extent that one is self-disciplined enough to follow those rules one can be guided and enlightened by the Holy Spirit to accurately handle the Word of God (2 Tim. 2:15; 1 John 2:27). However, even the Holy Spirit cannot or will not override the fleshly tendency to get caught up in a school of thought, or a doctrinal system, or a popular theory or trend, and engage in manipulating Scripture to support what one already has chosen to believe, or prefers to believe. And in fact, once one has been indoctrinated or influenced by other men whom they trust and respect, or has become excited about their own theories and ideas, it is very difficult to recognize the subjective elements of such an approach. But it is not so difficult to make the evidence that refutes those already formed conclusions, go away by rationalization. Perhaps this is why John gave us some of the promises and warnings that we see in the epilogue to this book:

> *"I testify to everyone who hears the words of the prophecy of this book: if anyone adds to them, God shall add to him the plagues which are written in this book; and if anyone takes away from the words of the book of this prophecy, God shall take away his part from the tree of life and from the holy city, which are written in this book."* (Rev.22:18-19)

1.2. The Timing of the Events Described in the Book of Revelation

With respect to the time frame about which John wrote there are again several different views. To a large extent the various views are largely related to the different approaches taken to interpreting Scripture, with considerable disagreement about the extent to which the book is prophetic.

1.2.1. The Various views on the Time-frame Addressed in the Book

The method of interpretation adopted will of course determine how one understands the book with respect to the time frame addressed in the book. As discussed briefly in the opening paragraphs of this chapter, the various schools of thought on this all-important factor generally seem to fall into one of four categories known as "Preterist," "Idealist," "Historicist," and "Futurist." Within these various camps are also divisions, such as Full versus Partial-Preterists, and Pre-tribulation versus Mid-tribulation and Post-tribulation Rapturists, and Pre-wrath Rapturists. As might be expected, these various schools of thought on the interpretation of Revelation correspond to doctrinal positions with regard to future things. Figure1.2.1 below presents an overview of these four major categories, and shows how they relate to various doctrinal or theological perspectives with regard to this whole subject of Eschatology. This figure appears in the Zondervan NIV Bible Commentary on this book of Revelation, where a description of each category is provided, which won't be reproduced here, except to briefly describe each. [11]

Theological Perspectives

	1 to 3	4 to 19	20-22
Postmillennial	Historic Churches	Generally historicist	Victory of Christianity over the world
Amillennial	Historic Churches	Generally historicist	Coming of Christ; judgment; eternal state
Premillennial	Historic Churches representative of historical stages	Generally futurist	Literal millennial reign; judgment of great white throne; New Jerusalem
Apocalyptic	Historic Churches	Generally Preterist	Symbolic of heaven and victory

Interpretations of Revelation

	1 to 3	4 to 19	20 to 22
Preterist	Historic Churches	Symbolic of contemporary conditions	Symbolic of heaven and victory
Idealists	Historic Churches	Symbolic of conflict of good and evil	Victory of good
Historicist	Historic Churches	Symbolic of events of history: fall of Rome, Mohammedanism, papacy, Reformation	Final judgment, millennium (?), eternal state
Futurist	Historic churches and /or seven stages of church history	Future tribulation; concentrated judgments on apostate church and on antichrist; coming of Christ	Millennial kingdom; judgment of wicked dead; eternal state

Taken from Wayne House, Chronological and Background Charts of the New Testament (Grand Rapids; Zondervan, 1978). Used by permission.

Figure 1.2.1

The allegorical approach to interpretation is obvious in the "Idealists"

---

11 Many individual theologians do not fall into any of these categories inasmuch as their interpretations would include more than one or a mix of two or more approaches such as partially historicist and partially futurists, or both idealists and Preterists or historicist to some degree.

understanding of the book, which spiritualizes almost everything and sees virtually no historical or predictive element in the book at all. According to them it is all about the struggle between good and evil, and teaches truths in the form of principles (moralizing), but has no bearing on any real world events. Thus with respect to time frames, it is the timeless approach.

The "**Preterists**" would see the events of Revelation as having occurred in John's own time, or shortly after he wrote it. To them the symbology of the Beast for example would have referred to the Imperial Roman government of that time. In this camp are the "Full Preterists" ("Radical Preterists") who see almost everything in the book as already fulfilled to the extent that we are living in the kingdom of God on earth today. Then there are the "Partial Preterists" ("Moderate Preterists") who see most of Revelation already fulfilled by AD 70, but admit that the some things such as the second coming and resurrection and judgment of the whole earth, are still future.

Similarly, the "**Historicists**" interpret the events in Revelation as having been mostly fulfilled already in history. While the Preterists and the Historicists are more literal in their interpretations than the idealists, they attempt to find its fulfillment in historical figures, for which the list of candidates is virtually infinite leading to so many different theories and scenarios as to render the whole discussion at best meaningless speculation, more confusing than enlightening.

Finally, there is the "**Futurists**" school, which sees most of Revelation as being prophetic of events that have not yet been fulfilled. Most of those who fall into this category see this book as apocalyptic literature that is predictive of the "end-times." The concept of "end-times" is based on literal interpretations of a great deal of Scripture (especially Daniel's prophecies) which predicts a time when Christ is going to return to judge the earth, and to save His own, and to set up a kingdom on this earth. This of course is also a theological position known as **Millennialism** - the belief that Christ's kingdom will be literally fulfilled on this earth. Many futurists also hold to the "**Premillennialists**" view that Christ's thousand year reign on this earth will not happen until after He returns to gather His elect to Himself, and to judge the whole world. A literal understanding of this book of Revelation, and such related passages as Matthew twenty-four and

1 Thessalonians 4-5 and 2 Thessalonians 1-2, make it difficult to hold to any other view, and support it scripturally.

It is the contention of this study that the reason why so many different and often incompatible interpretations of this book have been forthcoming down through the ages since it was written, even among those who attempt to understand it as literally as possible, is because of some combination of the following:

1) Poor exegesis, often more manipulation to fit a presupposition than objective analysis of the text;

2) Failure to take into consideration everything Scripture reveals on the given subject - as in other passages of Scripture, particularly Old Testament prophecy;

3) Ignoring the evidence that refute one's interpretation, selectively gathering only facts that support one's theory or interpretation;

4) Inattention to details - focusing only on those details that fit in with or support one's own scenario or theory;

5) Forcing Scripture to fit into one's preconceived system of theology and doctrinal positions, and even one's theological or cosmological theories, as opposed to letting Scripture speak for itself;

6) Failing to apply the disciplines of logic and either inductive or deductive reasoning, falling into circular reasoning, or accepting inconsistencies and contradictions in one's own interpretation.

This is by no means an exhaustive list of all the errors that have been made in the approaches men have taken to interpreting this book, but it does address some of the more subtle errors that seem to characterize most of the current literature on this subject.

As mentioned previously, an allegorical approach to understanding this book is herein deemed far too speculative and subjective to be worthy of any time or effort being devoted to it. If the Scripture has no literal meaning, which can be objectively evaluated and analyzed, then it isn't of any real value other than as intellectual entertainment perhaps for those who enjoy cosmic fiction or philosophizing. On the other hand, if it is God's inspired word then it is safe to assume that God is capable of communicating to us what He wants us to know, and doing it in a way that is not just confusing, nor wide open to speculation, nor designed to lead to controversy. However, as in the case of other documents of import, such as the Constitution of the United States, men are quite capable of distorting and misconstruing the message, imposing instead their own view on what the text says, and coming up with a wide variety of interpretations. As with the Constitution (to a lesser degree) the problem does not exist in the text itself. God has communicated clearly and His message is not garbled, or cryptic, or ambiguous, or open to speculation and individual interpretation. However, like any other piece of literature, it must be taken as literally as possible recognizing obvious symbolism and symbolic language when required by the text. It must be thoroughly studied to be sure that every text is taken in its proper context, letting Scripture interpret Scripture. It must be approached without bias and presuppositions as to what it can or should mean, letting the message and its meaning come from the overall text of Scripture itself. The disciplines of accepted rules of logic and deductive reasoning must be applied, including careful and honest exegesis, as opposed to subjective approaches to interpretation.

However, perhaps most importantly, in the case of the Bible one must be depending upon the Holy Spirit of God to be the teacher, and to enlighten one as to the message that God is trying to communicate. Studying Scripture is not meant to be <u>primarily</u> an intellectual exercise (though it is that) to develop one's own knowledge (though it accomplishes that), but it is to be a vital part of a living and vibrant relationship. That relationship is between the creator God, and His created children whom He loves enough to come and die for. It is not possible for a mere mortal with no more than human intellectual capabilities, to discern God's truth even from God's Word, without the enlightenment of the supernatural Spirit of God (see 1 Cor. 1:18-2:16, especially 2:9-14).

Probably this is in large part true because without the submission to and control of the Spirit of God no man can resist the temptation to read into the written text what he believes it should say. It is most natural, and indeed almost irresistible, to develop some kind of Cosmological or Metaphysical theory, or some kind of organizing principles, or to have some presuppositions or biases, before one even begins to actually read the Word of God. In most cases the reader is to a greater or lesser degree unaware of their own biases, and the fact that they have such presuppositions, or how much it is affecting their interpretive processes.

The more education one has, especially theological education or Bible training, the greater the presuppositions associated with the pre-indoctrination one has thereby received. This may occur formally as in a College or Seminary education, or informally as from reading Bible Commentaries and related books, or listening to sermons or tapes, or hearsay from others in the Christian community. This is especially true in the case of the prophetic books, and even more so in the case of Revelation. Because of the obvious difficulty in understanding the book, largely related to the extensive use of imagery and symbolism, the typical student of the book will quickly resort to other men's writings to try to find out what is going on in the book. Instead of taking the necessary time and effort (which is considerable, measured in terms of thousands of hours and years of intensive study of the whole Word of God) to gain the bigger picture, and to become sufficiently familiar with the text itself, and with its author, instead one resorts to quicker and easier approaches. Therein lies the rub - **the dependence is quickly and subtlety shifted from the Spirit of God and the Word of God, to whichever human sources one chooses to accept as authoritative**. Time spent in studying Revelation involves much more time reading or researching works about the book by other men, than actually studying the book itself and related passages of Scripture. Such an approach makes it very difficult at best, and almost impossible for a person to actually let the text speak for itself, as they already think they know what it has to be saying, and what it can't be saying. Even attempts to analyze the text exegetically become skewed and distorted by the bias one brings to the subject.

However, the man-made interpretations will show the fingerprints of the human element. Invariably the scenarios developed will involve discontinuities, contradictions, and illogical and/or impossible situations or events - especially with respect to this subject of Eschatology. They will involve omissions of relevant information provided in Scripture, or very forced revisions of relevant Scripture, and usually a large dose of eisegesis and invention - reading into Scripture things that aren't there. This will involve forced definitions of words and terms, which fit a certain theological perspective or system of theology, but do not come from either objective exegesis nor the natural use of the words or terms in the texts where they are used (a good case in point is the interpretations of the term "generation" as discussed above, or "the day of the Lord" as discussed in following discussions).

Another telltale technique is the co-mingling of interpretation with application, trying to define the meaning of a text in terms of an application. This is when the interpreter decides to whom a given text does or does not apply, and to what time frame or event the interpreter decides it must apply, when in fact the text itself does not indicate that such applications are necessarily intended (a case in point are the often repeated stipulations by some that "the Church is not in view" in the Olivet Discourse of Matthew 24, nor in Revelation 4-18).

Conversely, perhaps more common is the failure to recognize to whom a given text does apply, and to whom it does not apply, even though it is clearly enough indicated by the text (as in the very common practice of invoking Old Testament passages written specifically to and for Israel, applying them to New Testament Saints in the Church). This is simply a matter of taking a text out of context.

One must carefully examine oneself in approaching Scripture to at least be aware of one's own presuppositions, or biases, or pre-indoctrination - whether it be the assumption that there can be no supernatural element, or that Revelation must be understood historically or idealistically, or that it must be interpreted in light of a certain school of systematic theology, or in accordance with an organizing principle such as Dispensational Theology. Rather such suppositions and views and systems of theology and eschatology should come from the objective study of the text itself, kept in the context of the whole of God's revealed truth in His Word.

It is of course impossible to approach this subject, or for that matter any subject, without presuppositions and biases. This author has been thoroughly indoctrinated in the mainstream conservative evangelical school of thought including Pre-millennialism, Pre-tribulation Rapture theory, and Dispensational Theology. However, intellectual honesty requires that every principle or tenet that one brings to the study of this book must be carefully examined and evaluated for its validity in light of what one finds literally revealed in Scripture, taken as naturally as possible. This has led this writer to eye-opening experiences on many points of doctrine and eschatology. It has reinforced and substantiated His view on the literal approach to interpretation as being by far the best approach leading to the best and most meaningful results. It has strongly reinforced his belief that the Scripture, and in particular Revelation, is supernaturally inspired by God (verbal plenary inspiration view). It has also reinforced his previously held position of a belief in a literal Millennium, and Christ's return to rapture the church and to resurrect the Saints, before that Millennial age begins.

Such an approach has, however, completely failed to support his previously held belief in a rapture of the Church seven years before the second coming of Christ, such that she will not have to endure any of the trials and persecutions which this book of Revelation, and the prophecies of Jesus Himself (Matt. 24), warn us about. Such an approach to studying Scripture has supported some of what he was taught about interpreting Scripture in terms of dispensations, except for the dispensational imperatives concerning eschatology - such as the tribulation period being a time when God is only dealing with the nation Israel, and not the Church.

For those who have already decided that these are inviolable tenets, and even hermeneutic principles (rules of interpretation), what follows in this commentary will be pure heresy. However, that approach to understanding Scripture, and Revelation in particular, is exactly what has led to so much confusion, and controversy, and such impossible and self -contradictory theories with so little scriptural support as one sees in the Pre-tribulation Rapture theory, if one dares to examine and evaluate it objectively and critically (as is also done in the following).

This is not to say that those who disagree with the interpretations of this author are less spiritual, or even morally dishonest. It is to suggest, however, that many very godly men down through the ages, who are consciously well intended, many for whom this author has high regard and respect (such as Dr. Walvoord who is often cited in the following because of his reputation as a widely read and recognized authority on the subject matter), may have failed the test of intellectual integrity as defined in the preceding discussion. Both their views, and their techniques and methods of interpretation are challenged in the following.

1.2.2. The Declarations of the Writers of Scripture with Respect to the Time intended

In keeping with the approach to interpretation defined above as the preferred approach, we should begin the discussion about the intended time frame with a close look at what the text itself indicates. In the very first verse John tells us that he is writing about *"the things which must shortly take place"* (Revelation 1:1). Given the modern translations of this verse it would seem to indicate that the "Preterists" (the view that John wrote about contemporary events which occurred in his time, or shortly thereafter) view would be the preferred interpretation, or even the "Historicists" view would be preferred to the "Futurists" view. However, if we are to interpret the book at all literally we will have a real problem finding anything in history that even remotely resembles the cosmic catastrophe of the sixth seal, or the globally disastrous plagues and judgments on the earth of the seven trumpets and seven bowls, or the battle of HarMagedon (Armageddon), or the second coming of Christ to set up His perfect kingdom on this earth. To accept such approaches to understanding the book is tantamount to writing it off as grossly exaggerated and sensationalized descriptions of the actual events prophesied, or more realistically just the wild ravings of a grandiose mad man with a hyperactive imagination. Even a casual look at the book tells one immediately that most of the events and scenarios described therein have never occurred in all of human history.

This being the case the intellectually honest and diligent student will engage in a very essential aspect of analyzing any literary work that has been translated from another original language, especially works of antiquity, examining carefully the wording in the original language. In this case such analysis is quite enlightening, giving us a very different picture of what the author intended to communicate. A place to begin such analysis might be to look at a word for word translation of the Greek by a respected Greek scholar. Dr. Alfred Marshall renders the Greek text (from the 21st edition of Eberhard Nestle's *Novum Testamentum Graece)* as follows:

"things which it behooves to occur with speed."

Whereas the NASB translators chose to translate the Greek expression "en tacei" using the English word "shortly," perhaps Dr. Marshall translates it more accurately, "with speed." "Shortly" is more of an interpretation of the expression "with speed," than a literal translation of it. In fact, the Greek word *tachei* comes from the root word *tachos* which is translated "speed, quickness, swiftness, haste ... with speed" according to Arndt and Gingrich (Walter Bauer's Lexicon, second edition). While it is also possible to interpret it as referring to the imminence of an event, that is not a primary or necessary interpretation.

Dr. Leon Morris gives us a summary of the two possible interpretations of this phrase in the "Prologue" to his commentary on this book of Revelation:

"This could mean that the fulfillment is expected in the very near future. But we must also bear in mind that in the prophetic perspective the future is sometimes foreshortened. In other words the word may refer primarily to the certainty of the events in question. The Lord God has determined them and He will speedily bring them to pass. But speedily has a reference to His time not ours. With Him one day is as a thousand years and a thousand years as one day (2 Pet. iii.8). It is also possible that the term should be understood as 'suddenly', i.e. not so much 'soon' as 'without delay when the time comes'." (*The Revelation of St. John*, from the Tyndale New Testament Commentaries):

The Zondervan NIV Bible Commentary seems to take the first interpretation, which is probably the most widely accepted, explaining it as follows:

"'What must soon take place' implies that the revelation concerns events that are future (cf. Da 2:28-29, 45; Mk 13:7; Rev 4:1; 22:6). But in what sense can we understand that the events will arise 'soon' (GK G5443)? From the preterist point of view (see the introduction), all will take place in John's day. But we do not need to follow this interpretation of the book. In eschatology and apocalyptic literature, the future is always viewed as imminent without the necessity of intervening time (cf. Lk 18:8). 'Soon' does not, in other words, preclude delays or intervening events, as Revelation itself suggests. In ch. 6 we hear the cry of the martyred saints: 'How long, Sovereign Lord, holy and true, until you . . . avenge our blood?' They are told to 'wait a little longer' (vv. 10-11). Therefore, 'soonness' means imminency in eschatological terms." (Zondervan NIVBC)

Dr. John Walvoord, however, in his commentary on this passage, takes Dr. Morris' latter interpretation as being the correct one (though they do not agree on the overall interpretation of much of the rest of the book):

"The word 'soon' (en tachei; cf. 2:16; 22:7, 12, 20) means that the action will be sudden when it comes, not necessarily that it will occur in rapid succession (cf. Luke 18:8; Acts 12:7; 22:18; 25:4; Rom 16:20)." (Walvoord, "Revelation", *The Bible Knowledge Commentary*)

While it is true that there seems to be a sense of imminence being communicated repeatedly in other passages dealing with our expectation of the return of Christ and related end-time events, such is probably not the intended meaning of this phrase in this verse, or in the other passages in this book where almost the same phrase is used. We now have almost 2000 years since John wrote this, and one would be hard pressed to show that very many, if any of the prophesied events have really been fulfilled. However, we do see the explicit and rather clear indication in this book, and in related prophetic passages, that once the fulfillment begins to occur things will happen rapidly, and most of them will be fulfilled in short order. From Daniel we learn that the events described as the time of tribulation will mostly occur within a "week of years," which translates to seven years. And in fact the time of great tribulation is even spelled out in both Daniel and Revelation as a period of half that, 1290 days or 42 months. Thus, the latter interpretation adopted by Dr. Walvoord is clearly well supported by Scripture, and makes more sense in this context without the need for quite so much explanation and clarification. Nor does it open the door to other inferior methods of interpretation as discussed above.

John does give us more information on this subject, as we progress through this first chapter. In fact John tells us that the one whom He saw in the first scene of this incredible vision, which we know from his description was Jesus Himself, is dictating to John what to write, saying:

"Write therefore the things which you have seen, and the things which are, and the things which shall take place after these things."(Rev. 1:19)

Here we have a pretty good indication that the subject matter in this book is not only about things that were present or occurring during John's lifetime, though it begins with such things, but also deals with future events - *"the things which shall take place after these things."*

From this passage alone it would be possible to argue that Jesus meant the immediate future, to occur during what was left of John's lifetime or shortly thereafter, although that wasn't much time for so much to occur. Furthermore, as we read on in the book, and correlate what we find to other relevant passages of Scripture dealing with the same subject, it becomes clear that such an interpretation is not really feasible. Unless one allegorizes the text, or strips it of any real meaning by taking everything as purely symbolic such that the events described are never really supposed to occur, it is clear that these things have never happened in the history of the world, nor anything even close to what we see described herein. Thus, taken in the context of the rest of Scripture it is rather clear that Jesus was indicating to and through John that what was to follow was dealing with future events.

When we look at the gospels we find passages that obviously parallel much of what we see in this apocalyptic book, but is summarized briefly by Jesus, and is described as a response to the question, *"what will be the sign of your coming, and of the end of the age?"* (Matt. 24:3). In His answer He makes two references to "the end" (Matt. 24:6 and 13), and describes clearly His physical and visible return to earth, as well as the cataclysmic cosmic events involving the sun and moon and stars (Matt. 24:29). These same cosmic events were also prophesied by Joel (2:10, 30-31), and again by Peter (Acts 2:17-20), and we see them again in the sixth chapter of this book of Revelation. Peter referred to it as "the last days." Daniel, clearly describing the same time frame as we find in chapter eleven of this book, refers to it as "the end of time" (12:4), "the end time" (12:9), and "the end of the age" (12:13). Thus, once again, if we let Scripture interpret Scripture it seems to be quite clear that what John is writing about in this book is mostly looking forward to the end of this present age in which we live.

Furthermore, if one is at all aware of what is going on in our world today it is difficult not to see that things are happening globally that are clearly setting the stage for much of what John saw and described in this book, to happen rapidly. For the first time in almost 2000 years Israel is again a nation, and is the focus of worldwide attention. For the first time in the history of the world there is a worldwide movement called globalism,[12] with social, political, and economic pressure on all the nations of the world to unite and surrender sovereignty to a one-world government, with a centralized economy. This unprecedented globalism combined with a rapidly spreading acceptance of "relativism" has paved the way for the acceptance of a universal religion in which differences in belief systems acquiesce to the ethic of "tolerance," and religious people of different faiths worldwide are uniting in a spirit of "ecumenism."

Ironically, at the same time and in the midst of this global movement embracing the overarching ethic of "Tolerance" (the modern substitute for the biblical command to love God and love our neighbor as ourselves) there is a growing resentment and spirit of animosity toward both Jews and Christians around the world. This can be seen in the form of outward hostility internationally, especially in the Muslim world. But it is also evident in only slightly more subtle ways in the antagonism of the "political correctness" movement, using the liberal media and liberal judiciary and the public school system to militate against Christians and Jews in the western world, including our own United States. "Born again" Christians who preach the gospel that Jesus is the only way, are branded as being "intolerant," "religious bigots and fundamentalists." We are already seen as the enemy of the global movement for worldwide peace and unity. Is the stage not set for the Antichrist to set up his global economy and religious system, which will involve another attempt to rid the world of Christians and Jews?

There are two prophesied events for which we are still waiting (contrary to the Pretribulation Rapturists' self contradictory doctrine of "Imminence"), which will let us know that we may be in that seventieth week of Daniel. The first is the peace treaty, or covenant with Israel brokered by the world leader, which will be the Antichrist. The second is the rebuilding of the temple in Jerusalem - probably on the temple mount.

---

12 The modern "globalism" is new and unique in that it calls for all ethnic and national loyalties and sovereignties to be subjugated to a one world government, as opposed to one ethnic or national leader trying to subjugate all the rest under his/her rule – as with the Mongolian, Alexandrian or Roman empires, or Islam or Communism.

As of this writing no one has emerged as being clearly such a world leader who could accomplish that feat, and the Jews do not yet have clear control of, or have not asserted their control over the Temple Mount. However, the world today is united in an unprecedented way against a commonly recognized enemy - international terrorism, and the chief perpetrators of that terrorism are recognized as Muslim extremists. Arabic residents living in the state of Israel who have opposed Jewish immigration from the start, and have violently opposed her statehood ("Intifada"), who have adopted the name "Palestinians," are still trying to regain control with the openly declared goal of driving the Jews out of what they consider to be their homeland. Now under the names Palestinian Liberation Organization (PLO), and Hamas (a militant Palestinian Islamic organization), they are engaged in a war of terrorism and propaganda appealing to world opinion and international politics. They have been winning in the arena of international politics and world opinion, but their current engagement in acts of terrorism and their connections with international terrorists may change that trend with Israel gaining ground in the court of world opinion - which is all that prevents her from taking control of the temple Mount. Zionists in Israel will not be silenced or satisfied until that temple is rebuilt on what is believed to be its original site, the temple mount. Today it appears as if that may not be such a remote possibility.

Furthermore, after September 11, 2002, when the terrorists struck New York City and Washington DC, the world came together as never before. This included not only political alliances, and military alliances, but a surge in ecumenism as well. People from all different faiths are finding common ground, praying together and turning to God - whoever that God may be for them. Ironically, even though the unthinkable acts were motivated and carried out by religious zealots of the Muslim faith, the world is chanting the mantra that we dare not discriminate against Muslim's, and their religion of Islam, but must embrace them as equally respectable to any other religion. How close are we to a one-world religion that embraces all faiths - except of course Christianity and Judaism because they are deemed intolerant?

It appears that John claimed to be writing about events that were yet future to him, and the content clearly indicates that he was writing about end-time events that parallel what the prophets and apostles and

Jesus Himself preached and wrote about. It also appears from a look at recent history and current events that we have entered into or are rapidly approaching those days about which John wrote.

1.3. Rules of Interpretation

There are of course widely recognized rules of interpretation, or hermeneutic principles which, must be followed to be objective in our search for God's truth as revealed in His word. However, such principles must not be or include some form of doctrinal presuppositions themselves, as the whole point of hermeneutics is to avoid subjective approaches to interpretation in which we understand the words to mean what we have already determined they should mean based on our doctrinal presuppositions.

For the most part, the same rules that would be applied to interpretation of any work of literature should be applied to Scripture. In the case of Scripture however, we have the clear claim throughout that it is God who is the author, and the writers are merely His instruments. Hence though we have many books (66 considered canonical) by many human writers (over 40) they must all agree in every point even though they complement each other, since it is the one God who is inspiring what they wrote. Thus **the cardinal rule that any given text must be interpreted in light of its context includes the broader context of the whole 66 books**. Furthermore, since we begin with the presupposition that God is infallible and never contradicts Himself, **what we find in one passage must agree with what is explicitly revealed in any other passage**. Hence what we see in Revelation must be interpreted in such a way that it does not contradict what we find in Matthew or Isaiah or Ezekiel or Daniel.

Another presupposition that affects our interpretation is the definition of what is *canonical* and what is not. In this study it is assumed that the Apocryphal books are not inspired Scripture. It is also assumed that Divine revelation and inspiration of Scripture ended in the first century apostolic age, and only the written word of God included in the canon of Scripture is in fact authoritative as God's Word, as opposed to men's teaching and doctrines and traditions (i.e. ***sola scriptura* as opposed to progressive revelation, or the authority of church tradition**).

Beyond such basic hermeneutic principles and presuppositional assumptions there are rules of logic, which have been applied in this study in interpreting the words and phrases appearing in the various texts. They include the following:

- First let us establish a premise that seems reasonable and would probably be acceptable to anyone who is not determined to hold to some preconceived bias: when the exact same phrase is used repeatedly throughout Scripture which refers to an event or series of events, or refers to a point in time, we should **interpret that phrase consistently** as referring to the same event or events or point in time, unless the context in which it is used necessarily dictates otherwise. We need to remember that there is one author of Scripture, though many writers (if we accept the doctrine of verbal plenary inspiration, without which we have little grounds for any meaningful discussion of this present subject of eschatology and prophecy). Any author who would not conform to such a rule would either himself be quite confused, or would be the author of confusion, and there would be little reason to waste time attempting to understand his work, as no objective conclusions could ever be reached, and it would only give rise to many varied subjective opinions.

- Along the same line and clearly related would be a second premise which is so intuitively obvious that it should be unnecessary to mention it: **if we argue on the basis of sound exegetical principles for one meaning of a given Hebrew or Greek word, versus another meaning, we should not then adopt the other meaning when it suits our doctrinal purposes** (i.e. change the meaning from one text to another based on doctrinal presuppositions). Should we not be consistent in how we interpret a phrase, unless something in the proper exegesis of the text itself objectively requires that we accept varying interpretations?

- Another similar premise that we need to agree upon might be referred to as the **"principle of agreement"** between passages referring to the same prophetic events.

In other words, if the **descriptions in various passages of historical/prophetic events which are supposed to occur in a certain point in time, are substantially in agreement and coincide, especially if they are very unique or cataclysmic in nature, then they are referring to the same historical/ prophetic events, unless the context of a passage necessarily dictates otherwise**.

- A fourth premise is related to the previous and might be called the "**principle of non-agreement**," that if there are **irreconcilable differences** between descriptions which cannot be accounted for by intellectually honest analysis of the original language (exegesis) or analysis of the common use of the language employed, **then it is necessary to understand them as descriptions of different historical/prophetic events**. Similarly, if the scope or magnitude of the descriptions varies in any significant way then they are not descriptions of the exact same events, though they may have reference to more than one event, or they **may be referring to different stages of development of the same events**.

- We often see prophecies which had immediate significance contemporaneously, and had a **short-term partial fulfillment** in historic events that have already occurred, but were not completely fulfilled in scope and magnitude or with respect to certain details, and therefore have a **long-range or future significance and fulfillment**. This is quite consistent with the biblical use of types - using actual historical personalities and events as types (symbolic representations which are predictive and illustrative in nature) of personalities or events that are to occur at a later time. We see in Old Testament history various types of Christ (such as Ruth's "Kinsman Redeemer" Boaz, or Isaiah's "lamb"), and even types of the Anti-Christ which is yet to come (many Bible scholars see the prophecy of Daniel 11:31 as partially fulfilled in Antiochus IV Epiphanes, 175-164BC).

- Finally, here in Revelation we see evolving **events or developments that are progressive** over some period of time, and it would seem reasonable that **we might well be given descriptions of both the early and later stages of their development.** In such cases we would expect to see a change in scope and magnitude from local events and situations to more global effects of those events and the situation worldwide, especially in light of the nature of the events involved (i.e. the cosmic disturbances).

The following articulates the conclusions derived from the application of these and other widely accepted rules of exegesis and interpretation.

CHAPTER 2

DISPENSATIONALISM AND THE "DISPENSATIONAL PRINCIPLE"

As virtually everyone knows Christianity is a rather broad term which includes a rather wide range of differences in theological beliefs, mostly related to the variety of approaches taken to interpreting the Bible, which are discussed in Chapter one. As explained there, even amongst rather conservative evangelical Christians there are those who interpret Scripture as literally as possible, and others which subscribe to less literal approaches, such as the allegorical approach, especially with respect to prophecy. However, the division is not only over the interpretation of prophecy, but biblical history as well, with respect to how God has chosen to relate to man since He created them. Two major schools of thought are known as Covenant Theology and Dispensationalism. Of particular interest relative to the subject of this study is the Dispensational approach to Scripture, from which we get the Pretribulation Rapture Theory and the associated interpretations of end-time prophecy.

Perhaps one of the best and most concise definitions of "Dispensationalism" is the following:

Definition:

- A Dispensation - The system by which anything is administered. In Christian terms, looking back, it refers to a period in history whereby God dealt with man in a specific way. (Conscience, Law, Grace)

- Dispensationalism - A system of theology that sees God working with man in different ways during different dispensations. While 'Dispensations' are not ages, but stewardships, or administrations, we tend to see them now as ages since we look back on specific time periods when they were in force.
- Dispensationalism is distinguished by three key principles.
1. **A clear distinction between God's program for Israel and God's program for the Church.**
2. **A consistent and regular use of a literal principle of interpretation**
3. **The understanding of the purpose of God as His own glory rather than the salvation of mankind.**

Ok, what does this mean in layman's terms. Read on.

What about the Dispensations?

The key to Dispensationalism is not in the definition or recognition of a specific number of dispensations. This is a misunderstanding of the opponents of Dispensationalism. Almost all theologians will recognize that God worked differently through the Law than He did through Grace. That is not to say that salvation was attained in a different manner, but that the responsibilities given to man by God were different during the period of the giving of the Law up to the cross, just as they were different for Adam and Eve. The Jews were to show their true faith by doing what God had commanded, even though they couldn't keep the moral Law. That's what the sacrifices were for. When the apostle Paul said that as to the Law he was blameless, he didn't mean that he never sinned, but that he obeyed God by following the guidelines of the Law when he did sin, and animal sacrifices were offered for his sins by the priests in the temple. Salvation came not by keeping the law, but by seeing it's true purpose in exposing sin, and turning to God for salvation. The Jews weren't saved based on how well they kept the law, (as many of them thought) as that would be salvation by works. They were saved through faith in God, and the work of Christ on the cross was counted for them, even though it hadn't happened yet.

Dispensationalists will define three key dispensations, (1) The Mosaic

Law, (2) The present age of Grace, and (3) the future Millennial Kingdom. Most will agree about the first two, and Covenant theology will disagree about the third, seeing this as the 'eternal state'. (Since they don't see a literal Millennial Kingdom - the future literal fulfillment of the Davidic Kingdom.)

A greater breakdown of specific dispensations is possible, giving most traditional Dispensationalists seven recognizable dispensations.

1. Innocence - Adam
2. Conscience - After man sinned, up to the flood
3. Government - After the flood, man allowed to eat meat, death penalty instituted
4. Promise - Abraham up to Moses and the giving of the Law
5. Law - Moses to the cross
6. Grace - The cross to the Millennial Kingdom
7. Millennial Kingdom - A 1000 year reign of Christ on earth centered in Jerusalem"[13]

While Covenant Theology (the view held by many if not most Reformed Theologians) sees all of God's dealings with man as falling under one basic covenant of Grace, Dispensationalism divides God's dealings with man over time (past and present and future) into at least three, and most say seven periods characterized by different economies called Dispensations. They are popularly defined today by most Dispensationalists as: Innocence (Adam in Eden), Conscience (after the Fall), Human Government (beginning with Noahic Covenant), Promise (beginning with Abrahamic Covenant), Law (beginning with Mosaic Covenant), Grace (beginning with Christ's death and resurrection), and the future Millennial Kingdom (beginning with the second coming of Christ to earth).[14] Most see the seven year "Tribulation Period" as a transition period between the present age of Grace and the future Kingdom age, though Dr. J. E. Hartill (former

---

13 "Dispensationalism," http://www.endtimes.org/dispens.html

14 See C.I. Scofield's notes on Genesis 1:28 in his Scofield's Reference Bible.

professor of Hermeneutics at Northwestern College) identifies it as its own Dispensation, the seventh of eight.[15]

Dispensationalists believe that God's people are divided into two groups, Israel and the Church. Israel was of course God's chosen people in the Old Testament, but as Paul explains in Romans 9-11, she was temporarily rejected by God as His people and replaced by the New Testament Church, which included saved Israel (Jews) as well as Gentiles who come to God through Christ. However, this was temporary as the nation Israel is to be restored in the future (as prophesied by most of the Old Testament prophets to Israel) when Christ returns to establish His kingdom on this earth, after the Church is raptured out.

Conversely, many if not most Covenant Theologians contend that God has one people and while there were Old Testament saints, and New Testament saints, and they all make up His church - the Israel of today and of the future is the Church. As a result most Covenant Theologians do not accept the idea that there will be a literal Israel, and a literal earthly Millennial kingdom, apart from the spiritual kingdom which is present now in the form of Christ in the Church.

Whereas Dispensationalists interpret literally both Old Testament and New Testament prophecy concerning a future Millennial reign of Christ on earth in a New earthly Jerusalem, Covenant, or Reformed Theologians interpret much of Scripture allegorically, and prophecy in particular as very hyperbolic and symbolic, but not to be taken literally. Both are very much driven by their Theological presuppositions with respect to how they interpret Scripture, and hence their eschatological views reflect those presuppositions. While Covenant Theology associated with Reformed Theology, and the associated Amillennialism or Preterism, is certainly problematic for anyone who believes we should take Scripture as literally as possible, as discussed in the preceding paragraphs (Literal vs. Allegorical Interpretation), the focus in this discussion is **Dispensationalism.**

2.1 Strengths of Dispensationalism

There is much to be said for the Dispensational interpretation of Scripture. It is not a view that is spelled out explicitly in Scripture, but neither is any

---

15 See <u>Principle of Biblical Hermeneutics</u> by J. Edwin Hartill.

competing view which similarly breaks down and structures scriptural truth into an organized system of interpretation and theology - such as Covenant Theology. Both views see the various covenants that God made with men down through history, as key to such a system of interpretation, as pivotal transition points in how God has chosen to relate to and govern His creation. Both have a lot of similarities in how they understand and interpret those covenants. To compare and contrast the two and attempt to evaluate their strengths and weaknesses in general is beyond the scope of this study, and there are already volumes written on the subject. We will focus on those aspects that relate to our subject matter at hand - end-times prophecy.

In an age after AD 70 (when the Roman General Vespasian completely destroyed Jerusalem) when there was no nation Israel, and no sign of her return to significant status as a national entity, prophecy that was about the nation Israel and her restoration in the land seemed quite unbelievable. Hence, even though the premillennial interpretations were predominant in the early church before Augustine, it is understandable that brilliant scholars, such as Philo, Clement and Origen (all of Alexandria) would find a way to interpret Scripture such that it would make more sense to them, and be more believable. Hence the allegorical school of interpretation was developed. Augustine applied it to apocalyptic prophecy, and it became the mainstream view for centuries. This method of interpretation was applied to the interpretations of the covenants, in particular the New Covenant versus the Old Covenant of the Mosaic Law, which of course applies to the definitions of "the Church" versus "Israel" in this present Church age. To the Covenant Theologian today, which includes most Reformed Theologians, there is no "Israel" as distinct from the Church, inasmuch as the references to Israel in the New Testament are taken allegorically rather than literally - even with respect to her restoration as God's people. This was the mainstream view even up to and beyond the Reformation.[16]

In light of these trends in the church down through the centuries to move away from the literal interpretation of Scripture toward more

---

16 It is confusing if not ironic that the protestant reformation involved a repudiation of the allegorical interpretation of Scripture in favor of a literal approach, yet those who call themselves "Reformed Theologians" today adhere to a form of the more allegorical approach with respect to the prophetic passages.

allegorical approaches, perhaps we owe a debt of gratitude to such men as Pierre Poiret (1646-1719) and John Edwards (1639-1716), and Isaac Watts (1674-1748), and John Darby and the Plymouth Brethren (mid 1800s),[17] for returning to a more literal approach to understanding Bible prophecy. These early Dispensationalists brought at least the mainline conservative evangelical element of Christianity back to the understanding that what God promised to the nation Israel is still applicable to the nation Israel. They revived the belief that Christ will return to earth and will reign on this earth for a literal thousand-year period. Based on their approach, we now have many teachers and preachers and theologians who believe that these end-times prophecies are about future events, which will be literally fulfilled, and therefore have real significance and meaning to us today.

Though there are several variations in the Amillennialists and even the Preterists interpretations, most tend to interpret the end-time and apocalyptic prophecies as having been largely fulfilled by AD 70 with the destruction of Jerusalem. They interpret most prophetic passages as being hyperbolic and figurative language not intended to be taken literally, but do insist on what they contend is a more literal interpretation of the prophecies of Jesus and writers of the New Testament epistles, with regard to the imminence of the fulfillment of those prophecies (such as "this generation shall not pass till all these things be fulfilled") - as discussed in the preceding Chapter 1. Such claims cry out for more careful analysis of the words used in the original language - which is also covered in the preceding chapter.

---

17 "The first person on record to develop a genuine dispensational scheme in a systematic fashion was the French philosopher Pierre Poiret (1646-1719). In his work entitled "The Divine Economy: or An Universal System of the Works and Purposes of God Towards Men Demonstrated," Poiret developed a scheme of seven dispensations covering the scope of Scriptures and history. This work was published in Holland in 1687. In 1699 John Edwards (1639-1716) published a well-developed dispensational scheme in his book entitled <u>A Complete History or Survey of All the Dispensations</u>. Isaac Watts (1674-1748 A.D.), the famous hymn writer and theologian, presented a system of six dispensations in an essay named "The Harmony of all the Religions which God ever Prescribed to Men and all his Dispensations towards them." During the 19th century the Plymouth Brethren, including one of their key leaders, John Nelson Darby (1800-1882), played a very significant role in developing, systematizing, and spreading Dispensational Theology." (Showers, R., Ancientpath.net, "Introduction to Dispensationalism.")

While the allegorical approach was originally adopted to make the prophetic Scriptures more believable, in light of developments in the last two centuries it is that same allegorical school of interpretation that has become less believable. The Covenant or Reformed Amillennialists' and Preterists' claims that all the clear prophecies about Israel being regathered in her home land as a nation again, are only really about the church and not about Israel at all - appear to be a little out of touch with experiential reality. And the interpretation that all of the apocalyptic prophecies that clearly involve not only the whole world but the heavens as well, are really only about the destruction of tiny Jerusalem in AD 70, lack surface validity - i.e. they seem absurd to the critical thinker. Then when we see the globalization that is actually happening, with the same people groups and even some of the same nations identified by Daniel exploding on the scene as powers to be reckoned with - it is hard not to see literal interpretations of these prophetic passages being fulfilled before our very eyes. Hence, it seems that the Dispensationalists have done a much better job of keeping up with the global developments of the 19th and 20th century and now into the 21st century, because of their more literal approach. Thus it is no surprise that the more literal approach of the Dispensationalists should be receiving more attention and respectability in the light of the many relatively recent historic developments.

2.2 Problems with Mainstream Dispensationalism

While the Dispensationalists have kept up with developments of the 19th and much of the 20th century because of their more literal approach - such as recognizing ethnic Israel among other developments as prophetic events - their failure to be consistent in applying that approach, and to keep up with evolving developments, has resulted in significant errors both logically and scripturally. Scripturally unsupportable presuppositions of the Dispensational System of Theology have led them to engage in eisegesis and forced interpretations of a number of key prophetic passages and certain critical aspects of Revelation. The result is a false scenario that is deceptively optimistic and escapist in nature, which may well account for much of its popularity with modern Evangelicals. Unfortunately such mistakes may have serious consequences for those actually living in those last few years when the most intense developments are happening rapidly and they fail to recognize them for what they are because they have been led to believe that they will be raptured out before such events are to occur.

Some theologians and Bible commentators often tell us that many passages of Scripture dealing with certain subjects (such as the Gog/Magog rebellion found in Ezekiel 38-39 and Revelation 20) are very difficult to understand. And indeed they are, if one approaches them with a whole set of doctrinal presuppositions, and an *a priori* mental construct and system of theology, into which these passages must all fit. Dr. Pentecost, while claiming to adhere to a strictly literal approach to interpreting Scripture as "The Essential Basis of the Pretribulation Rapture Position," has to add a qualifying statement, which is very revealing:

> "Pretribulation rapturism rests essentially on one major premise - the literal method of interpretation of the Scriptures. **As a necessary adjunct** to this, the pretribulationist believes **in a dispensational interpretation** of the Word of God." (emphasis added)[18]

Unfortunately reading the explanations and commentaries of these brilliant men it becomes clear that the "adjunct" takes precedence over the literal interpretation when it comes to passage after passage - which is why it is deemed so "necessary." The result is a set of conflicted and contradictory explanations, and very illogical scenarios that are neither themselves internally consistent, nor are they consistent with the Scripture, as demonstrated many times in the following commentary presented in this Thesis.

Certainly understanding Scripture is not easy in the sense that a lazy or casual or undisciplined approach to studying it will not be rewarded with a correct and comprehensive explanation of things to come. The subject matters being dealt with, such as God's purposes, and His methods in dealing with man, are rather complex issues involving a lot of underlying spiritual realities, which are by no means obvious to fleshly creatures. Dispensationalism, like Reformed Theology, is an attempt to systematically define and articulate some of those spiritual realities, and is up to a point quite scriptural. However, like all man-made systems of thought, it has its limitations. As applied to Eschatology, principles have been defined and

---

18 Pentecost, Things to Come, XIII, I., p. 193.

articulated which sound good, and sound very pious and spiritual, but often tend to either fall short, or go beyond what Scripture literally teaches.

Perhaps the main reason why we have so many different eschatological views and such a variety of interpretations and explanations of the same book is because people become informed and indoctrinated into a system of theology, or a certain school of thought, before they become thoroughly familiar with the Word of God. As they read and study the Scripture, they are always interpreting what they read in light of what they already know and believe to be true. They then fall into the trap of finding a way to make each passage of Scripture fit into their preconceived construct, and they ignore those passages which they can't make support their view. In reality, the system of theology that they adopt becomes a rule of interpretation, an overriding hermeneutic, if you will. At least Dr. Pentecost is being honest in this regard.

In the case of Dispensationalism one former professor of Hermeneutics refers to what he calls "The Dispensational Principle," making the following bold assertion:

> "Unless one understands the dispensations, one cannot understand God's Book, and it becomes a Book of confusion and contradictions." (J. Edwin Hartill, <u>Principles of Biblical Hermeneutics</u>, chapter Two, p. 13)

In his text book Dr. Hartill then defines these "Dispensations" as including the seven identified above, with the addition of "The Dispensation of Judgment or Tribulation." This additional dispensation is defined as beginning with the rapture of the Church before the beginning of the "seven year tribulation period" - the 70th week of Daniel. With this in mind as a principle of interpretation, it is not difficult to see how his students would come to the conclusion that Scripture is teaching a pretribulation rapture - every verse has to be interpreted according to this rule of interpretation. This is how we get passages such as Matthew 24 and 2Thessalonians 1 and 2 being interpreted to support such a position, a position which is actually refuted by those very passages when taken literally in their natural sense.

Even if Dispensationalism were 100% completely true, to use it as a rule of interpretation would be a very misguided and intellectually dishonest approach to interpreting Scripture. It is in fact the very kind

of subjective approach that the whole science of "Hermeneutics" is designed to preclude. Such an approach leads the Covenant Theologian to come up with different interpretations on the same passages of Scripture as those being considered by the Dispensationalists, and both will be equally valid given the rules of interpretation followed by each respectively.

The fact is that like Covenant Theology, Dispensationalism is itself clearly an interpretation, as is the Pretribulation Rapture position, and it is what proponents of those views are actually trying to prove. To begin with presuppositions assuming that they are facts, then interpreting every Scripture in such a way that they all conform to those presuppositions, is a perfect example of "**circular reasoning**" or "arguing from one's premise." Such an approach proves nothing other than the blind dedication and commitment of the adherent to the system of theology to which they feel compelled to conform, which they are determined to prove or defend no matter what.

On the other hand, it is true that one must make certain assumptions, and understand certain principles, in order to make sense out of the Bible as a whole, and especially prophecy concerning the latter days and end times. God has dealt differently with man throughout different periods of history, and obviously has a plan to change things in the future. Thus it is necessary to understand some of these principles to make sense out of Scripture. However, it becomes critically important that the derivation of such principles actually comes from the literal interpretation of Scripture derived from an objective approach, with rules of interpretation that are not merely a restatement of a system of theology or eschatology. Such rules must preclude forced interpretations of passages of Scripture, and rather allow the Scripture to speak for itself. They should require one to allow Scripture to explain Scripture, rather than resorting to man-made theories and systematization.

The student of Scripture who wishes to find God's truth is best served if he or she can become aware of all the presuppositions and assumptions with which they are approaching Scripture. They should consider them all to be just what they are - assumptions and presuppositions, until one has found them explicitly articulated in Scripture, following objective rules of interpretation. Each set of constructs or scenarios or conclusions one draws should be evaluated using the only tools that we have to protect us from falsehood and error - rules of logic and deductive or inductive reasoning.

The same rules that we would apply to our opponents' views must be applied just as rigidly to our own constructs, theories and conclusions.

If these principles were indeed followed consistently by people studying the Bible, it is very likely that there would be much less division and disagreement, with fewer denominations and cults all claiming to be Bible believing Christians. Unfortunately they are not often followed, and the result is what we have today - so many interpretations one can't keep track of them all. It is this author's contention that it is not Scripture that is so obscure. An honest, objective approach, under the guidance of the Holy Spirit, will lead honest truth seekers to very similar, if not the same conclusions. If we strip away the artificial barriers and constraints that we unnecessarily place upon our perception of what Scripture is saying, it is surprising how much becomes clear, even logical and believable.

Are we really to believe that God intended to so encrypt His communications with men, such that only an elite group of professional theologians and clerics (such as Seminary graduates in full-time ministry) are capable of decoding it? While it may seem to them to be in their best interest (job security) to have Scripture be so obscure, such that only they can comprehend and decode it, is this not the thinking of the Pharisees of Jesus' time, or the Roman Catholic hierarchy of the Dark Ages? Did God intend that men should be dependent upon some hierarchy of human scholars to accurately communicate to the common lay Christian? Surely Scripture is clear enough that we are not supposed to be dependent upon scholarly men - an elite class amounting to a modern day "priesthood" - who alone have the keys to understanding Scripture. That is the stuff of cults.

Clearly God has given spiritual gifts of knowledge and discernment to some men (1 Cor. 12:4-10), and has given men with such gifts as gifts to the church (Eph. 4:7-11). But just as clearly He has warned us against putting our faith in men telling us instead to be relying upon the Holy Spirit within us to guide us into all truth as we look to the source document, His Word, for the answers (John 14:26; 16:13; 1 John 2:27). While Revelation is obviously very symbolic, and its truths are not accessible to the intellectually lazy, or those who are biblically illiterate, neither do they require one to first subscribe to a preconceived theory or a doctrinal position developed by men, but nowhere explicitly taught in Scripture.

The Dispensational system of Theology, and in particular the Pretribulation Rapture theory, have been developed by men trying to organize Scripture in a way that makes sense to them. No one can honestly claim that either is explicitly stated in Scripture, though inferences may be drawn from Scripture, which are interpreted so as to support such positions. However, to the critical thinking person who approaches Scripture objectively, it is quite clear that such positions are not only **not** entirely supported by explicit Scripture, and do not always enhance the understanding of Scripture, but rather are in some points contradicted by explicit Scripture, and involve glaring discrepancies logically speaking. The fact is that Scripture does explain Scripture without the need to engage in the kind of circular reasoning and questionable exegesis as demonstrated and discussed above, and in the following.

2.2.1. Problematic Presuppositions of Dispensationalism

There are several presuppositions associated with Dispensationalism, and its daughter the Pretribulation Rapture (PTR) view, which determine their interpretations of Scripture on the subject of end-times prophecy, and drive their conclusions. They include an assumption about the whole purpose for the Tribulation Period, and who is to be involved in and affected by it. They also include axiomatic declarations of *a-priori* assumptions with respect to what the key passages on the subject can or cannot be saying, with respect to who will be involved in and affected by the Tribulation Period, and who will not. Some of these presuppositions are addressed in the following.

2.2.1.1 The Tribulation Period is only for judgment on Israel - not for trying and testing the Church

One of the important tenants of the version of Dispensationalism to which most self-identified Dispensationalists subscribe, is the presupposition that God's dealings with the Church end at the beginning of the Tribulation Period (the 70th week of Daniel). He is only dealing with Israel during that seven-year period. The logic is that God's program for Israel is laid out in the Old Testament [19] - and especially in Daniel nine where time frames

---

19 See Dwight Pentecost's <u>Things to Come</u> as a representative and exhaustive presentation of this view.

are given - and the church is not going to be a part of that program at any time. The reasoning seems to be that since the rest of the Old Testament eras, the first sixty-nine weeks of Daniel's prophecy, dealt only with Israel (since the church age had not arrived yet), therefore the seventieth week must also involve only Israel. This of course means that the church must be raptured out before the seventieth week begins.

One problem with this assumption is that unlike the fact of the seventieth week and its events, which are explicitly articulated as fact in Scripture, nowhere are we told that the church cannot be present on earth when God resumes His program with Israel during that seventieth week. This doctrinal tenet is nothing more than a deduction on the part of some men, which they then assume to be true, but cannot demonstrate from Scripture (and seldom even attempt to do so apparently because they feel it is so logical).

Although most do not see the seven year Tribulation Period as a separate dispensation from the Church Age, or the Age of Grace (Dr. Hartill being a notable exception), they nonetheless insist that there is a major shift in God's dealings and relationship with men, from Church centered to ethnic Israel centered. They maintain that it is a period in which God is judging and purifying only His original chosen people - the nation of Israel.

Scriptures that would clearly seem to indicate that the church is present during this period, undergoing persecution as well as judgment and purification, are explained away. One of the most common explanations given is that such passages can't possibly be about the church since the church has already been raptured out at the beginning of that period (another presupposition - arguing from their premise). Then they in turn argue that since the church is not present during that period and God is only dealing with Israel, that means that the church has already been raptured out before the period begins (blatant circular reasoning).

There is no Scripture taken literally that even suggests that God is only dealing with Israel during that 70th week of Daniel - this is an assumption invented by men, a "Dispensational Principle." In fact, as we read the New Testament prophecies about this period, Revelation in particular, there is actually little mention of Israel, except for the 144,000 of Revelation 7 and 14, the temple and the "Holy City" of chapter 11, and the "Woman" of chapter 12. Ironically the mention in that 12th chapter tells us the she will actually be supernaturally protected by God for 1260 days, not judged. Few would argue or even suggest that the "New Jerusalem" of chapter 21-22 is about Israel, as the future heavenly scene is described there. But we do see the Saints throughout which are being tested and tried and martyred - who are they, unbelieving Israel? Certainly not! This is a glaring discrepancy in the Dispensational Principle.

Of course the Dispensationalists have an answer to that question - they are the "tribulation Saints" - not the church, but people who have come to Christ after the Church has been taken out. However, the only basis for making this distinction between these "tribulation Saints" and the Church, is the presupposition that the Church had to be raptured out before all of this began - with **no explicit Scripture to support that claim**.

Only in an environment of comparative ease and lack of opposition such as we enjoy in America, which is unique in the history of the Church, could anyone seriously contend that God would not allow His Church to go through the testing and persecution described in Revelation. One might ask the early church, the Apostles who died as martyrs, or the suffering Church around the world today, if this is a valid presupposition. And if we do accept such a premise, how would this same God then be allowing those faithful "Tribulation Saints" to go thru it all, as Scripture clearly indicates He will? [20] Again we have another logical contradiction.

To suggest that the Tribulation Period doesn't have anything to do with the Church is to ignore the salient fact that the book of Revelation opens with three chapters to the churches, chapters two and three actually naming specific churches. The one message repeated to each of those churches is that they must overcome and endure to the end. In the exhortation to one of those churches, Philadelphia, reference is made specifically to "the hour of testing ... which is about to come upon the whole world" (Rev. 3:10) - which is widely understood by Dispensationalists as referring to

---

20 The answer given may be that God lets those "Tribulation Saints" go through what He would never let the Church go through, because they missed the rapture - the Pretribulation Rapture, which is nowhere mentioned as such in Scripture. So for those who came to Christ one day or second later than others who get raptured, it is ok for them to go through what is unthinkable for God to let the earlier converts go thru. Good luck trying to find that principle stated in Scripture, or understanding the logic of it.

this Tribulation Period. To then insist, as they do, that these first three chapters really have nothing to do with the rest of the book, as there is really a rapture of the church between the 3rd and 4th chapter - though no mention is made of it there (or anywhere else in Scripture) - is very disingenuous at best, intellectually dishonest. Those two opening chapters are in fact an introduction to the following apocalyptic visions, precisely as one might expect, to warn the church that she will be tried and tested, and even judged. Such testing and judgment will be consummated at the end of the age just before Christ returns to rescue them and to judge the rest of the world.

Of course, Revelation 3:10 has to be explained away to overcome that hurdle, and they are quite up to the task. By doing exactly what they often accuse their opponents of doing, they simply come up with their own definition of a key word in that passage, the little proposition which in the Greek is *ek* (ek). By doing the same kind of linguistic trick used in Matthew 24 with the word "elect," (discussed below), they force the verse to say what fits with their presuppositions - again, intellectually dishonest. This also will be discussed further in the following.

2.2.1.2 The Church is Not in Matthew 24

A prime example of presuppositions dictating interpretation is the case of the popular interpretations of Matthew 24. Advocates of the Pretribulation Rapture position (which I will call PTR) must emphasize and repeatedly warn the reader that "the church is not in Matthew 24." That is without doubt because the unindoctrinated reader who takes Matthew 24 at face value without presuppositions, will very likely understand it to be saying that saved believers - "the elect" - will be going thru very trying times, descriptions of which parallel the events described in Revelation. Then, according to Matthew 24:29-31, "after the tribulation of those days," immediately before the catastrophic "sixth seal" cosmic event referred to as "the sign of the Son of Man," they will be raptured out.

> [29] *"But immediately* **after the tribulation of those days** *the sun will be darkened, and the moon will not give its light, and the stars will fall from the sky, and the powers of the heavens will be shaken.* [30] *And then the sign of the Son of Man will appear in the sky, and then all*

the tribes of the earth will mourn, and they will see the Son of Man coming on the clouds of the sky with power and great glory. [31] *"And He will send forth His angels with a great trumpet and they will* **gather together His elect** *from the four winds, from one end of the sky to the other." (Matthew 24:29-31)*

However, Dispensationalists emphatically insist that the "elect" in Matthew 24 refers to saved Israel (see Pentecost, Things to Come), or only Tribulation Period Saints, not just all saved believers, and not the church. The problem is they never interpret the "elect" as Israel or Tribulation Period Saints anywhere else where the same word is used (other than born again Jews which are part of the Church). In fact they understand Israel to be the "branches" of the "olive tree" of Romans 11:16-24 which are "broken off" - i.e. temporarily rejected by God in favor of the Church. Nowhere in the New Testament do we see Israel referred to as "the elect." Even in the one case where Israel is the topic of the discussion, Romans 11:5-7, the "chosen" only refers to the "remnant" of Israel which are saved by accepting Christ, which are part of the Church.

They attempt to support this contention with logical arguments, which are not necessarily so logical when examined critically, unless one simply accepts unquestioningly the presupposition that the Tribulation Period is a time when God is only going to be dealing with Israel (as insisted upon by Pentecost). Unfortunately, as we have already pointed out, such a premise is nowhere stated in Scripture. Nor for that matter is it implied in Scripture, when taken literally in its most natural sense - in fact the opposite is indicated, especially in Revelation, as we will demonstrate in the following. Aside from that they simply revert to circular reasoning, that since the church has already been raptured out before the tribulation period, the "elect" here in Matthew can't be the church, hence the church must not be in Matthew 24.

Bible scholars who subscribe to this Dispensationalists PTR interpretation that this text is not written to or about the church tell us that Matthew was written mostly to a Jewish audience, as opposed to Mark and Luke, which were more for the Gentile readers. However, with the exception of this 24th chapter, they all apply the rest of what is written in this Gospel to the church, such as the Great Commission of

Matthew 28:19-20, or the "Beatitudes" of the Sermon on the Mount of chapter 5, or the Lord's Prayer of chapter 6, or such often cited passages as Matthew 6:33, 10:38-39, 11:28, and many other parables and passages and teachings which are clearly as much for the Gentile church as are any of the other Gospels. Furthermore we have the parallel passages in the other Gospels, Mark 13 and Luke 17 and 21, which are supposedly written to the Gentiles, which have the same warnings and promises, including this promise about the "elect" being raptured out:

> *"24But in those days, after that tribulation, the sun will be darkened and the moon will not give its light, 25and the stars will be falling from heaven, and the powers that are in the heavens will be shaken. 26Then they will see the Son of Man coming in clouds with great power and glory. 27And then He will send forth the angels, and will* **gather together His** **elect** *from the four winds, from the farthest end of the earth to the farthest end of heaven." (Mark 13:24-27)*

Would they also have us to believe that Mark 13 is only written to and about saved Jews? Perhaps not but they still contend that it is only referring to the Israel, or the "tribulation Saints," who will come to Christ after the rapture of the church, during the Tribulation Period. But the only rationale for such an interpretation of Mark 13 is their presuppositions - their "dispensational distinctive" or hermeneutic that the rapture just has to happen before the Tribulation Period begins - again, with no explicit Scripture or logical arguments to support that presupposition.

The reality is that Matthew 24 is an excellent proof text for the contention that the Church will **not be raptured out before the Tribulation Period begins**. The "elect" here is the same as it is anywhere else in the New Testament where the term is used - it is the Church. The contention that it is a prophecy about the second coming of Christ is of course quite accurate. That is exactly when the Saints alive at that time will be raptured out, before God pours out His wrath on the Antichrist and his followers. But the contention that it is not the church because the church had already been raptured out seven years earlier, has **no scriptural support - not one verse**.

It might be noted that it is this gathering together of His elect which they contend is only the second coming of Christ, which is also what is referred to in this passage, as well as those other passages, which tell us that it will come when no one is expecting it because no one knows the day or the hour:

> *[36] "But of that day and hour no one knows, ...Therefore be on the alert, for you do not know which day your Lord is coming. ... for the Son of Man is coming at an hour when you do not think He will."* *(Matthew 24:36-44)*

This is an important tenet of the PTR view, related to their doctrine of "imminence," discussed in the following in chapter 4. Yet, if, as according to their view, the church is suddenly all taken out seven years before this second coming event, how will this occurrence be so imminent and unknown - one need only calculate seven years from that rapture event to know exactly what day that second coming will happen. Hence again we have another example of contradictions associated with this interpretation. They can't have it both ways - if this "imminent" event is not the rapture but a separate event that happens seven years after the rapture, then it is not really an imminent event at all. It only makes sense to say that it is imminent - such that no one will know the day or the hour - if it is indeed the rapture as well as the second coming of Christ. The reality of course is that it is the rapture which is imminent and cannot be predicted, and it is the second coming of Christ which is also imminent and cannot be predicted because the rapture and the second coming are concurrent events.

2.2.1.3 The Church is Not in Revelation

Here we go again - what works for Matthew 24 should work for the book of Revelation. At least the approach to reaching such a conclusion is about the same. By assigning the right definitions to the words used in the text, and applying circular reasoning, we can make the case for the presupposition that "the Church is not in Revelation." Exactly as they must do for Matthew 24, they also must do for the whole Apocalypse.

Probably the mainstream teaching among Dispensationalists is the contention that Christ is going to return to rapture out the church before the seven years of tribulation begin. However this does present them with a problem in that **we do actually see the Church throughout the whole book of Revelation**. We see that there will be a body of saved believers, who are following Christ, being persecuted by the Beast, the Antichrist, and his False Prophet (12:17; 13:7; 14:12). We see this same body of believers who have remained faithful to death appearing dressed in white robes before the throne of God in heaven, where we are told that they have "come out of the great tribulation" (Rev. 7:9-17). And finally, we see them resurrected and reigning with Christ during the Millennium after being martyred for refusing to worship the beast (Rev. 20:4). These are simply referred to as "saints," or those who "have washed their robes and made them white in the blood of the Lamb" (7:14), or those who "keep the commandments of God and hold to the testimony of Jesus" (12:17), or as those who persevere and "keep the commandments of God and their faith in Jesus" (14:12). Certainly if there were any possible way to indicate or describe the church it could not be better articulated than it is in these passages. By definition "the Church" is the body of believers who have put their faith and trust in Jesus, have been washed in His blood, obey His commandments, and hold to His testimony (never deny Him), and persevere in their faith to the end. What else could we add to define and describe the church?

Strangely enough, the mainstream teaching among conservative evangelicals who are literalists and futurists, is that "**the church is not in Revelation**" after the third chapter. This is like a mantra that is repeated over and over again by those who teach that the rapture of the church must happen before the beginning of the Tribulation Period. Of course they do have to qualify this a little bit, as even they have to admit that the church is undeniably appearing at the "marriage of the Lamb" of 19:7 (though incredibly some even parse this text and words so as to deny that she is present at the "marriage supper of the Lamb" in that same passage (19:9)) [21]

The only rationale given, or textual evidence cited to support this contention that the church is not in Revelation 4-18 is the fact that the Greek word translated "church" does not appear in that part of the book. And in fact it does not appear again after the third chapter until the last chapter in 22:16 – not even in the 19th thru the 21st chapter where the same men would insist the church does appear even though the word for "church" (ekklesia) does not appear there either.

This would seem to be a most disingenuous argument inasmuch as the

---

21 See Pentecost's discussion of "The Marriage of the Lamb" in his book Things to Come.

word church does not appear in 8 of the New Testament books, nor in the Gospels of Mark, Luke or John, or in 1 John or 2 John or 1 Peter or 2 Peter or Jude. Surely no one would even suggest that the church is not in these other New Testament books because the Greek word translated "church" does not appear there. Jude uses the word "saints" to refer to the church, which appears 12 times in the part of Revelation where we are told the church does not appear. **The fact of the matter is that John doesn't use the word "church" in any of his works, except in Revelation.** For that matter he doesn't use either word, "church" or "saints" to refer to saved believers in his other works (the Gospel of John and the three epistles) but his descriptions match exactly what we see in Revelation – those who confess Jesus is the Son of God and who obey His commandments and overcome by faith (1 John 3:24 & 4:15 & 5:4-5).

It would be far more honest and accurate to acknowledge that John didn't really use this word to refer to the body of Christ, except when he was referring to specific local assemblies as in the 2nd and 3rd chapters of this book of Revelation. In fact in most cases throughout the Bible where the word is used it is used to refer to specific "assemblies" of believers, or what should be going on in those assemblies when they are gathered together. When referring to the "church" in general, the body of believers, other words are normally used throughout Scripture- such as "saints," "the bride," and "the elect." Hence the fact that it is not used much in Revelation is certainly no indication that the church is not there. This is simply a perfect example of the kind of intellectually dishonest manipulations to which men resort when they are trying to force interpretations of Scripture to fit presuppositions and preconceived theories or doctrinal positions.

Indeed there is nothing in Scripture when translated accurately and interpreted literally, taking the most natural and obvious meaning of the text in light of its context, which suggests that the church in Revelation is anything other than "the Church." Only the presupposition that the Church has to be raptured out before the events prophesied in the book begin to occur would lead one to the notion that the Church in Revelation is not really "the Church," the "elect," the "bride of Christ," as it is in any other book of the New Testament. But for one to hold to that preconceived belief it is necessary to explain away all the appearances of the church in the rest of the book – no matter how forced such interpretations may be.

2.2.2 Problematic Methods of Interpretation of Mainstream Dispensationalism

As we have seen above, not only is there a problem with presuppositions, but ironically the strength of Dispensationalism is proving to also be its downfall. While bringing us back to the **literal interpretation of Scripture**, which has made it much more meaningful and believable in today's world, they have allowed their presuppositions to undermine that commitment to literalism. In the passages discussed above, very unnatural and imprecise exegesis and interpretation of key words allow them to modify (or subvert) the meaning of the text to force it to say what they believe it should say. That the order of events in Matthew 24 parallel those of Revelation would seem to be unmistakable, and that they are part of what is to take place during the Tribulation Period is undeniable. That they are said to be occurring before the rapture is even more clear, unless we say that the rapture of Matthew 24 is not the same rapture as that of 1 Corinthians 15:51, 1 Thessalonians 4:14-5:10, and 2 Thessalonians 2. This is a common device used to make Scripture say something it doesn't really say without some help. It not only involves coming up with a definition or interpretation of a word that is linguistically and exegetically unsubstantiated, but also committing the fallacy of making a distinction when there is none. Nowhere does Scripture indicate that there is more than one rapture, but PTR Dispensationalists have come up with two - to get around the obvious message of Matthew 24. They do the same thing with the references to the Church in Revelation, the second coming of Christ, and other more obvious issues such as the "day of the Lord" (especially in 2 Thessalonians 2), the word "*ek*" in Revelation 3:10, and Gog/Magog of Ezekiel 39-39 and Revelation 20. Whenever the text refutes or disagrees with their theories and scenarios, they simply change the text - works every time.

2.2.2.1 Revelation 3:10

As mentioned briefly in the preceding paragraphs, the forced interpretation of Revelation 3:10 is a prime example of either very poor scholarship, sloppy exegesis, or intellectual dishonesty. Taken literally, a word for word translation of this verse per Marshall's Interlinear, is as follows:

"Because thou didst keep the word of the endurance of me, I also will keep out of the hour of trial being about to come on the inhabited [earth] all, to try the [ones] dwelling on the earth." (Rev. 3:10 Marshall's Interlinear New Testament)[22]

According to many of the proponents of PTR theory, such as Tim LaHaye, this phrase "keep you from the hour of testing," is virtually proof that Scripture teaches that the Church will be raptured out before the seven year tribulation period begins. And indeed, if the interpretation of those who agree with LaHaye is the best or only interpretation of this phrase based on good exegesis of the Greek text, then they may have a credible argument (as long as we take it out of context of everything else the Bible teaches about this gathering of the elect). However, at the risk of being considered a modern day "heretic," one might want to evaluate their interpretation of that phrase.

Perhaps the explanation given by David Levy in his book <u>Revelation Hearing the Last Word</u> [23] is one of the more lucid and yet brief articulations of this interpretation and the argument derived from it:

> "The Lord gave this church a promise of protection: 'Because thou hast kept the word of my patience, I also will keep them from [out of] the hour of temptation, which shall come upon all the world, to try them that dwell upon the earth' (v. 10). Many people teach that the church will go through a portion or all of the Tribulation mentioned in Revelation 6-19, but the language of this verse makes it clear that the church will not go into the Tribulation. This *hour of trial* will be a time when God's wrath will be poured out upon the world. Several things verify this fact.
>
> 1. The preposition *from* (Gr., *ek*) means *out of*; that is, *out of the midst of*, a clear indication that the church will not go through any portion of the Tribulation. If the writer meant to say that the church was going *through* tribulation, he could have used a different Greek preposition, *dia*.

---

22 Marshall, Alfred, <u>NASB-NIV Parallel New Testament in Greek and English, with Interlinear Translation by Alfred Marshall</u>.

23 Levy, David, <u>Revelation: Hearing the Last Word</u>, pp. 55-56.

2. This is not just any trial, but *the hour of trial*, a specific season of Tribulation that is coming. ..."

The author goes on to make three more points, which are mostly based on his interpretation and the related arguments made in these first two points. However, the question is, is this an accurate interpretation of the words in question, based on good and honest exegesis?

First one needs to examine the word cited here as the crux of the issue. Is it true that the Greek word "*ek*" means "out of the midst of" with the connotations that Mr. Levy has ascribed to it? According to respected Greek scholars such is not the case. First a quick look at a lexicon informs one that this preposition "*ek*" has a wide variety of possible English words which accurately translate it, depending upon how the word is used. Thayer's Lexicon gives us five major categories; Walter Bauer's (Gingrich, Arndt, and Danker) Lexicon gives us six major categories, with numerous subcategories for each. When we see the variety of words used to translate this Greek word, as can be quickly observed from a glance at The Englishmen's Greek Concordance of the New Testament, we realize that this is not a word which has one simple meaning, and excludes all others, as implied by Mr. Levy's argument.

Of course, as is always the case, the proper translation can in part be determined from the context, and even the grammatical context, meaning we have to look at the combination of words being used here. Then, keeping it in the context of the whole of Scripture, and letting Scripture explain Scripture (as opposed to opinionated men and brilliant human scholars), we can look at other passages where the same combination of words are used, and from this we can gain insight as to what acceptable interpretations of those words may include.

In this case a renowned and highly respected Greek scholar, who is not unfriendly to the pre-tribulation rapture view, gives us an honest exegetical look at the use of this word in this passage. Dr. A.T. Robertson points out that this word "*ek*" is used here in conjunction with the word "*tereo*" translated "*will keep*," and then cites another passage where the same construction is also used. That other passage is quite revealing with regard to the claims made above by Mr. Levy, and LaHaye and many other theologians who have written on this subject:

"I do not ask Thee to take them out of the world, but to **keep them from** *the evil one." (John 15:17)*

Here we find the exact same word, and the same grammatical construction. Could anyone argue from this passage that the words "**keep them from**" means to take them out of or away from "the evil one" such that they will not be exposed to or be in any way tempted by, or attacked by him? If Jesus was praying for a "keeping from" in that sense, as men like Levy insist is the way it must be taken in our text in Revelation, then He was praying against what Scripture tells us was, is and will be the case. If this was what Jesus meant His prayer was very ineffectual in that His request has certainly not been granted. Jesus Himself told Peter that this same "evil one" was attacking him, and trying to sift him like wheat. Peter tells us that the devil is like a roaring lion seeking to devour us, whom we have to resist (1 Peter 5:8-9). Paul tells us that our warfare is against the spiritual forces of darkness, and specifically mentions the "flaming missile of the evil one" (Eph. 6:12-17). Thus, clearly the words "**terero ek**" do not necessarily mean to keep from as in the sense of "**out of the midst of**," meaning that they will not be exposed to that from which they are being kept. In fact, taken in context, Jesus is clearly saying that those for whom He is praying will be exposed to the very trials and temptations that He is asking God to protect them from. Clearly He is praying for their protection in the sense that they will be victorious, overcomers, when tried and tested and tempted by that same evil one (and indeed, that request by Jesus on their behalf was ultimately granted).

Similarly, in our text the words are being used in exactly the same way as they were in John 17:15. Even the issue is very similar, in that what God is promising here is that when this hour of trial comes upon the whole world, God is the one who will enable them to be the overcomers - which is the reoccurring theme throughout these two chapters of this book of Revelation. If the church was to be taken out of the world, overcoming and persevering would not even be an issue, much less the main theme of the text (another logical contradiction in their interpretation).

Dr. Robertson is not alone in his understanding of these words. Another respected and often cited Greek scholar, M.R. Vincent makes the following observation:

"From the hour (ek). The preposition implies, not a keeping from temptation, but a keeping in temptation, as the result of which they shall be delivered out of its power. Compare John xvii. 15." (Vincent, <u>Vincent's Word Studies of the New Testament</u>, "Revelation of John," p. 466.)

Here, from the same Greek word we see Dr. Vincent drawing the exact opposite conclusion as that reached by Mr. Levy. However, like A.T. Robertson, he does so based on his examination of the other passage which he also cross-references, the John 17:15 passage discussed above.

Another renown Bible commentator and Greek scholar, Henry Alford, who is also sympathetic to the pre-tribulation rapture view, gives his honest evaluation of this Greek word as follows:

"from (from out of the midst of: but whether by *immunity from*, or by *being brought safe through*, the preposition does not clearly define)". (Alford, <u>New Testament for English Readers</u>, "Revelation," p. 1809).

Thus, as Alford points out, one cannot make a clear statement about what this passage in Revelation means, based solely on the preposition used. On the other hand, when we let Scripture interpret Scripture, as opposed to a presupposed system of theology (such as Dispensationalism) and a preferred eschatological view (such as Pretribulation Rapture theory), one would surely lean towards renown Greek scholars Dr. Robertson's or Dr. Vincent's interpretation as opposed to Dr. Levy's, or Dr. LaHaye's, who have no such reputation as authorities on the Greek – perhaps for obvious reasons.

However, even proponents of the PTR view are not all ignorant of the problems and issues discussed above. Dr. Walvoord, former president of Dallas Theological Seminary, often cited as one of if not the leading expert on this subject of Eschatology, and an ardent advocate of the PTR view, in his commentary on this passage makes the following admission:

"Other instances of the use of the same verb and preposition together, such as John 17:15 and James 1:27, would indicate that it is perhaps too much to press it to mean an absolute deliverance." (Walvoord, <u>The Revelation of Jesus Christ</u>, p. 87)

However, Walvoord then goes on to argue that it must be understood as "absolute deliverance from" in light of everything else this book has to say about this "tribulation period." Of course, what he means is that he believes we should interpret this verse in a way that fits in with his interpretation of the rest of the book. [24] What he fails to do here, unlike Robertson and Vincent above, is give another passage of Scripture to support his contention. As we study further in this book, and examine his interpretations of it, we find other interpretations which involve very similar approaches to interpreting many other passages - very lacking in literal scriptural support but clearly driven by a preconceived doctrinal position (Dispensationalism and Pretribulation Rapture Theory).

2.2.2.2 The "Day of the Lord"

Perhaps the most consequential, and hence most unfortunate deviation from the literal approach to interpreting Scripture using accepted rules of hermeneutics and exegesis is what the Dispensationalists have done with the phrase "The Day of the Lord." In fact, so significant is this error that a whole chapter is devoted to it in the following.

Whereas Scripture is clear that this phrase refers to a day of Judgment on the earth when Christ will return to execute that judgment, PT Rapturists would tell us that it actually means the whole seven years of the Tribulation Period, and the following 1000 years of the Millennium as well. Only by adopting such an interpretation of the word can they make so many passages of Scripture conform to their presupposed scenario, with two comings of Christ and a rapture before the Tribulation Period. This is discussed in depth in the following chapter entitled "The Day of the Lord."

---

24 This is another example of circular reasoning, or using an interpretation of a text to support a view which view is itself used to support the interpretation of that selfsame text.

CHAPTER 3

"THE DAY OF THE LORD"

Many of the passages which make definitive statements about Christ's return to rapture out the Church and to judge the earth, use the phrase "the Day of the Lord." It is used to denote something very specific and very significant. It is also quite well defined from all the various contexts in which it is used, in both Old and New Testament prophecies. Hence there is really no excuse for misunderstanding or misinterpreting it - unless one defines it based on presuppositions instead of letting Scripture define it, using good exegesis.

After defining what the term means, particularly with respect to how it is used in Scripture, we will look at how men have defined it.

3.1 The Definition of "the day of the Lord"

Perhaps a pivotal point, and a vital key to understanding and tying together the various Scriptures with respect to the subject of the second coming of Christ, or the rapture, or the resurrection, or the judgment of God on the earth, is to correctly discern the meaning of the expression "the day of the Lord." The conclusions reached about the timing of the rapture of the Church, and other eschatological issues, will depend largely upon how we understand this phrase. Before we can say how the passages in Matthew 24,[25] 1st and 2nd Thessalonians, or 2 Peter 3, and such key Old Testament passages as Joel 2, are related to each other or to our text in Revelation, we

---

25 Even though Matthew 24 does not use this exact expression it is clearly about this future day when Christ returns to judge the earth and rescue His people.

need to address this critical question: exactly what is Scripture referring to when it speaks of "the day of the Lord"?

However, before we attempt to determine the meaning of this key phrase, we need to remind ourselves of the objective rules of interpretation which we will follow. These are discussed in the introduction, but we will briefly reiterate them here:

- First we need to be consistent in our translation and interpretation of words - such as the word "day." We don't change the meaning from one text to another unless the context dictates otherwise.
- Secondly, when the exact same phrase is used repeatedly throughout Scripture which refers to an event, or series of events, or a point in time, we should interpret that phrase consistently as referring to the same event or set of events, or times, unless the context in which it is used necessarily dictates otherwise.
- Similarly, if the descriptions in various passages of historical/ prophetic events are substantially in agreement and coincide, especially if they are very unique or cataclysmic in nature, then they are probably referring to the same historical/prophetic events, unless the content or context of a passage necessarily dictates otherwise.
- Conversely, if there are irreconcilable differences between descriptions which cannot be accounted for by intellectually honest analysis of the original language (exegesis) or analysis of the common use of the language employed, such as when the scope or magnitude of the descriptions vary in any significant way, then it is necessary to understand them as descriptions of different historical/prophetic events.

If we apply these rules to the interpretation of the expression, "the day of the Lord," it leads us to certain conclusions. However, not everyone complies with such rules, and from this comes no end of confusion, and disagreement, and debate, as discussed in the following.

3.1.1 The "day of the Lord" as Used in Scripture

Following an essential rule of interpretation, we will begin by examining how this expression, "the day of the Lord," also sometimes rendered "the day of God," is used in Scripture. This is not really that difficult as it is only used 23 to 25 times, depending upon which version one chooses (KJV 25, NIV 24, and NASB 23 times). The following are the relevant texts in which this expression is used:

> *"Behold, the* **day of the Lord** *is coming, cruel, with fury and burning anger, To make the land a desolation; and He will exterminate its sinners from it. For the stars of heaven and their constellations will not flash forth their light; the sun will be dark when it rises, and the moon will not shed its light." (Isaiah 13:9-10)*

> *"Wail, for the* **day of the Lord** *is near! It will come as destruction from the Almighty. Therefore all hands will fall limp, and every man's heart will melt. And they will be terrified, pains and anguish will take hold of them. They will writhe like a woman in labor, they will look at one another in astonishment, their faces aflame. Behold, the* **day of the Lord** *is coming, cruel, with fury and burning anger, to make the land a desolation; and* **He will exterminate its sinners from it***. For the stars of heaven and their constellations will not flash forth their light; the sun will be dark when it rises, and the moon will not shed its light. Thus I will punish the world for its evil, and the wicked for their iniquity; I will also put an end to the arrogance of the proud, and abase the haughtiness of the ruthless. I will make mortal man scarcer than pure gold and mankind than the gold of Ophir. Therefore I shall make the heavens tremble, and the earth will be shaken from its place at the fury of the Lord of hosts in the day of His burning anger."(Isa.13:6-13)*[26]

---

26 In context this is a prophecy that concerns an invasion by Babylon, thus some Bible commentators interpret it as referring only to the historic events with no eschatological significance. To do so, however, they have to ignore the striking similarity of the language and metaphors used with that of other passages which they do interpret as prophetic of the end time apocalypse - passages such as Joel 2:31 and 3:14, Matthew 24:29, Acts 2:20, and Revelation 6:12. Clearly the details of vv. 9-13 of this prophecy by Isaiah have never been fulfilled - hence the dual nature of prophetic passages (near term partial fulfillment, long-range future complete fulfillment) also applies in this case, as in most other prophetic passages.

"For the day is near, even the **day of the Lord is near**; *it will be a day of clouds, a time of doom for the nations." (Ezek. 30:3)*

"Alas for the day! For the **day of the Lord** *is near, and it will come as destruction from the Almighty." (Joel 1:15)*

"Blow a trumpet in Zion, and sound an alarm on My holy mountain! Let all the inhabitants of the land tremble, for **the day of the Lord** *is coming; surely it is near, a day of darkness and gloom, a day of clouds and thick darkness. As the dawn is spread over the mountains, so there is a great and mighty people; there has never been anything like it, nor will there be again after it to the years of many generations. A fire consumes before them, and behind them a flame burns. The land is like the garden of Eden before them, but a desolate wilderness behind them, and nothing at all escapes them. Their appearance is like the appearance of horses; and like war horses, so they run. With a noise as of chariots they leap on the tops of the mountains, like the crackling of a flame of fire consuming the stubble, like a mighty people arranged for battle. Before them the people are in anguish; all faces turn pale. They run like mighty men; they climb the wall like soldiers; and they each march in line, nor do they deviate from their paths. They do not crowd each other; they march everyone in his path. When they burst through the defenses, they do not break ranks. They rush on the city, they run on the wall; they climb into the houses, they enter through the windows like a thief. Before them the earth quakes, the heavens tremble, the sun and the moon grow dark, and the stars lose their brightness. And the Lord utters His voice before His army; surely His camp is very great, for strong is he who carries out His word. The* **day of the Lord** *is indeed great and very awesome, and who can endure it?" (Joel 2:1-11)*

"And I will display wonders in the sky and on the earth, blood, fire, and columns of smoke. The sun will be turned into darkness, and the moon into blood, before the great and awesome **day of the Lord** *comes." (Joel 2:30-31)*

"Multitudes, multitudes in the valley of decision! For **the day of the Lord** *is near in the valley of decision. The sun and moon grow dark,*

and the stars lose their brightness. And the Lord roars from Zion and utters His voice from Jerusalem, and the heavens and the earth tremble. But the Lord is a refuge for His people and a stronghold to the sons of Israel." *(Joel 3:14-16)*

"Alas, you who are longing for the day of the **Lord**, for what purpose will the day of the **Lord** be to you? It will be darkness and not light; as when a man flees from a lion, and a bear meets him, or goes home, leans his hand against the wall, and a snake bites him. Will not the day of the **Lord** be darkness instead of light, even gloom with no brightness in it?"*(Amos 5:18-20)*

"Near is the great **day of the Lord**, near and coming very quickly; listen, the **day of the Lord**! In it the warrior cries out bitterly. A day of wrath is that day, a day of trouble and distress, a day of destruction and desolation, a day of darkness and gloom, a day of clouds and thick darkness, a day of trumpet and battle cry, against the fortified cities and the high corner towers. And I will bring distress on men, so that they will walk like the blind, because they have sinned against the Lord; and their blood will be poured out like dust, and their flesh like dung. Neither their silver nor their gold will be able to deliver them on the **day of the Lord's wrath**; and all the earth will be devoured in the fire of His jealousy, for **He will make a complete end, indeed a terrifying one, of all the inhabitants of the earth**." *(Zeph. 1:14-18)*

"Before the decree takes effect-- the day passes like the chaff-- before the burning anger of the Lord comes upon you, before **the day of the Lord's anger** comes upon you. Seek the Lord, all you humble of the earth, who have carried out His ordinances; seek righteousness, seek humility. Perhaps you will be hidden in the **day of the Lord's anger**." *(Zeph. 2:2-3)*

"Behold, I am going to send you Elijah the prophet before the coming of the great and terrible **day of the Lord**. And he will restore the hearts of the fathers to their children, and the hearts of the children to their fathers, lest I come and smite the land with a curse." *(Mal. 4:5-6)*

"And it shall be in the last days, God says, 'that I will pour forth of My

Spirit upon all mankind ... And I will grant wonders in the sky above, and signs on the earth beneath, blood, and fire, and vapor of smoke. The sun shall be turned into darkness, and the moon into blood, before the great and glorious **day of the Lord** *shall come." (Acts 2:17-20)*

"For you yourselves know full well that the **day of the Lord** *will come just like a thief in the night. While they are saying, "Peace and safety!" then destruction will come upon them suddenly like birth pangs upon a woman with child; and they shall not escape." (1 Thess. 5:2-3)*

"Now we request you, brethren, with regard to **the coming of our Lord Jesus Christ,** *and* **our gathering together to Him,** *that you may not be quickly shaken from your composure or be disturbed either by a spirit or a message or a letter as if from us, to the effect that* **the day of the Lord** *has come. Let no one in any way deceive you, for it will not come unless the apostasy comes first, and the man of lawlessness is revealed, the son of destruction, who opposes and exalts himself above every so-called god or object of worship, so that he takes his seat in the temple of God, displaying himself as being God." (2 Thessalonians 2:1-4)*

"But the **day of the Lord** *will come like a thief, in which the heavens will pass away with a roar and the elements will be destroyed with intense heat, and the earth and its works will be burned up. Since all these things are to be destroyed in this way, what sort of people ought you to be in holy conduct and godliness, looking for and hastening the coming of the day of God, on account of which the heavens will be destroyed by burning, and the elements will melt with intense heat!" (2 Pet. 3:10-12)*

As we read these passages, and all of the other passages which refer to this "day of the Lord," we see only one theme and that is **judgment.** And in fact it is not just another of many judgments on Israel or on her enemies, but a unique judgment that is universal and thorough with a clear note of finality. Isaiah tells us that sinners will be exterminated from the land (Isa. 13:9), and Zephaniah tells us that **"He will make a complete end, indeed a terrifying one, of <u>all the inhabitants of the earth</u>" (Zeph. 1:18).** In fact Zephaniah begins his prophecy by telling us that God said He would "completely remove all things from the face of the earth" (Zeph. 1:2). He also refers to this same day of judgment as "the day of the Lord's wrath" (Zeph. 1:18), or "the day of the Lord's anger" (Zeph. 2:2 & 3), which certainly seems to correlate to what John is writing about in Revelation 14:19, 16:17-21, and 19:15, which passages are clear references to the second coming of Christ in judgment on the earth. It also seems to correlate to what Peter tells us in the passage cited above, that in that "day of the Lord" the heavens and the earth are going to be "burned up ... the heavens will be destroyed by burning, and the elements will melt with intense heat!"

Several passages tell us about the signs in the heavens which will mark the arrival or beginning of this day of judgment. According to Isaiah this day is a day of "wrath and fierce anger", and is directly associated with the cosmic disturbances:

> *"Behold, the* **day of the Lord** *is coming, cruel, with fury and burning anger to make the land a desolation; and He will exterminate its sinners from it.* **For the stars of heaven and their constellations will not flash forth their light; the sun will be dark when it rises, and the moon will not shed its light**. *Thus I will punish the world for its evil, and the wicked for their iniquity; I will also put an end to the arrogance of the proud, and abase the haughtiness of the ruthless. I will make mortal man scarcer than pure gold, and mankind than the gold of Ophir. Therefore* **I shall make the heavens tremble, and the earth will be shaken from its place** *at the fury of the Lord of hosts in the day of His burning anger." (Isa. 13: 9-13)*

Similarly, both Joel, and Peter (as recorded by Luke in Acts), refer to the same cosmic events, which Jesus also prophesied in the Olivet Discourse (Matt. 24:29; Luke 21:25):

> *"But immediately after the tribulation of those days* **the sun will be darkened, and the moon will not give its light, and the stars will fall from the sky, and the powers of the heavens will be shaken**, *and then the sign of the Son of Man will appear in the sky, and then all the tribes of the earth will mourn, and they will see the Son of Man coming on the clouds of the sky with power and great glory. And He will send forth His angels with a great trumpet and*

they will gather together His elect from the four winds, from one end of the sky to the other." (Matt. 24:29-31)

These cosmic events would seem to match, and find fulfillment in one rather major future event, the sixth Seal of Revelation 6:12-17:

"And I looked when He broke the sixth seal, and there was **a great earthquake***; and the* **sun became black as sackcloth made of hair, and the whole moon became like blood; and the stars of the sky fell to the earth, as a fig tree casts its unripe figs when shaken by a great wind. And the sky was split apart like a scroll when it is rolled up; and every mountain and island were moved out of their places***.** *And the kings of the earth and the great men and the commanders and the rich and the strong and every slave and free man, hid themselves in the caves and among the rocks of the mountains; and they said to the mountains and to the rocks, 'Fall on us and hide us from the presence of Him who sits on the throne, and from the wrath of the Lamb; for* **the great day of their wrath** *has come; and who is able to stand?'" (Revelation 6:12-17)*

This event will involve the obscuration of the sun and other heavenly luminaries, cause the moon to appear blood red, and will feature meteor showers, or comet strikes like we have never seen. It will involve earthquakes that will level mountains, and even the heavens will "tremble" (see also Joel 2:10 & 30-31 and Matthew 24:29 cited above). This is a huge, major, global and cosmic disaster, which no living thing will survive, except those supernaturally saved and protected by God.

This "day of the Lord" is about judgment for the world, and only judgment. It is not primarily about the regathering of Israel and her restoration physically or spiritually (though a remnant will repent at that time and be saved) - that will mostly happen after God has finished this final judgment on His people. It is a day which we are warned will come like a **thief in the night** <u>for those who aren't watching and aren't prepared for it</u>. However, Jesus also told us that we should be watching, and that we should see the signs and be prepared. He warned us that no one will know the day or the hour (Matt. 24:36), but that we will have plenty of signs - just as the budding of trees in spring tell us summer is coming, so we will know when "He is near, right at the door" (Matt. 24:32-33).

Between these prophecies, including what Jesus said, it becomes clear when this "day of the Lord" is to occur with respect to other end-times events. Isaiah and Joel have made it quite clear that the "day of the Lord" will be preceded by the cosmic sign events discussed briefly above (this is discussed in considerable detail in a companion work entitled The Seals, Trumpets and Bowls of Revelation Revisited). Thus we know that what John is describing in the sixth chapter of Revelation will happen before that same "day of the Lord," or as that day of judgment commences. However, Jesus also told us that these cosmic sign events will happen "immediately after the tribulation of those days" (Matt. 24:29), which we see from the context is referring to the time of "great tribulation." Jesus tells us that this is also the coming of the "Son of Man" - which we refer to as the second coming. What Jesus said seems to agree perfectly with what Paul wrote to the Thessalonians on this subject:

> *"Now we request you, brethren, with regard to* **the coming of our Lord Jesus Christ**, *and* **our gathering together to Him**, *that you may not be quickly shaken from your composure or be disturbed either by a spirit or a message or a letter as if from us, to the effect that the* **day of the Lord** *has come. Let no one in any way deceive you, for* **it will not come unless the apostasy comes first, and the man of lawlessness is revealed**, *the son of destruction, who opposes and exalts himself above every so-called god or object of worship, so that he takes his seat in the temple of God, displaying himself as being God." (2 Thessalonians 2:1-4)*

So once again we have very clear indications explicitly stated in God's Word as to what this "day of the Lord" is, and when it is going to occur (see Figure 3.1.1-1). It will happen after the time of great tribulation has already been going on, and after the beast of Revelation (the "antichrist") has appeared on the scene and has desecrated the temple and set himself up as God. It will also begin immediately after the signs in the heavens, the cosmic events of the sixth Seal of Revelation. It coincides with Christ's return to this earth, coming on the clouds of the sky with power and great glory, and His gathering together His elect from the four winds (Matt. 24:27-31; see also 2 Thess. 2:1-3). It is the day of God's judgment on the whole earth, and it coincides with Christ coming again to earth.

3.1.2 The "Day of the Lord" as Popularly Defined by Many Dispensationalists

There are just about as many definitions of this term as there are major views on the end times, and in fact those very definitions play a key role with respect to how men interpret end-time prophecy. A comparison of these views and their definitions of the "Day of the Lord" as well as the "Day of Wrath" are depicted in figure 3.1.2-1. The main focus of this study however is on the Pretribulation Rapture versus the Posttribulation Prewrath Rapture views (Figure 3.1.2-2).

A popular explanation of this term, "the Day of the Lord," as it is used in 1 Thessalonians five, is given by former Dallas Theological Seminary professor Thomas Constable, as follows:

> "The **day of the Lord** is a future period of time in which God will be at work in world affairs more directly and dramatically than He has been since the earthly ministry of the Lord Jesus Christ. It is a time referred to by many Old Testament prophets (e.g., Isa. 13:9-11; Joel 2:28-32; Zeph. 1:14-18; 3:14-15). As these and other Old Testament verses indicate, **the day of the Lord will include both judgment and blessing**. That day begins immediately after the Rapture of the church and ends with the conclusion of the Millennium. This day is a major theme of prophecy with its fullest exposition in Revelation 6-19." (Thomas Constable, "1 Thessalonians", <u>The Bible Knowledge Commentary - An Exposition of the Scriptures by Dallas Seminary Faculty</u>, edited by John F. Walvoord and Roy B. Zuck, Victor Books, 1983, p. 705 (highlight added))

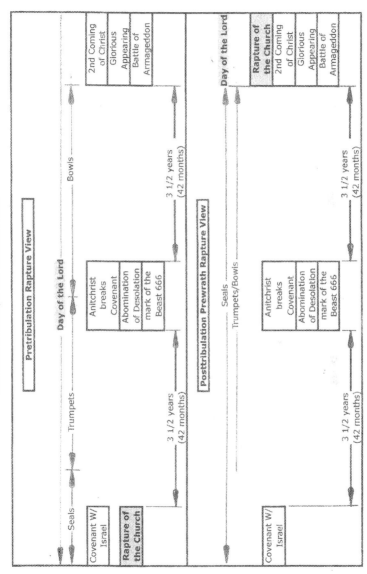

70th Week of Daniel / 7 Year Tribulation Period

Pretribulation Rapture View

Day of the Lord

Bowls

2nd Coming of Christ
Glorious Appearing
Battle of Armageddon

Anitchrist breaks Covenant
Abomination of Desolation
mark of the Beast 666

Trumpets

Seals

Covenant W/ Israel

Rapture of the Church

3 1/2 years (42 months)

3 1/2 years (42 months)

Posttribulation Prewrath Rapture View

Day of the Lord

Rapture of the Church

2nd Coming of Christ
Glorious Appearing
Battle of Armageddon

Trumpets/Bowls

Seals

Anitchrist breaks Covenant
Abomination of Desolation
mark of the Beast 666

Covenant W/ Israel

3 1/2 years (42 months)

3 1/2 years (42 months)

Comparison of two Views
Pretribulation vs. Postribulation Prewrath Rapture

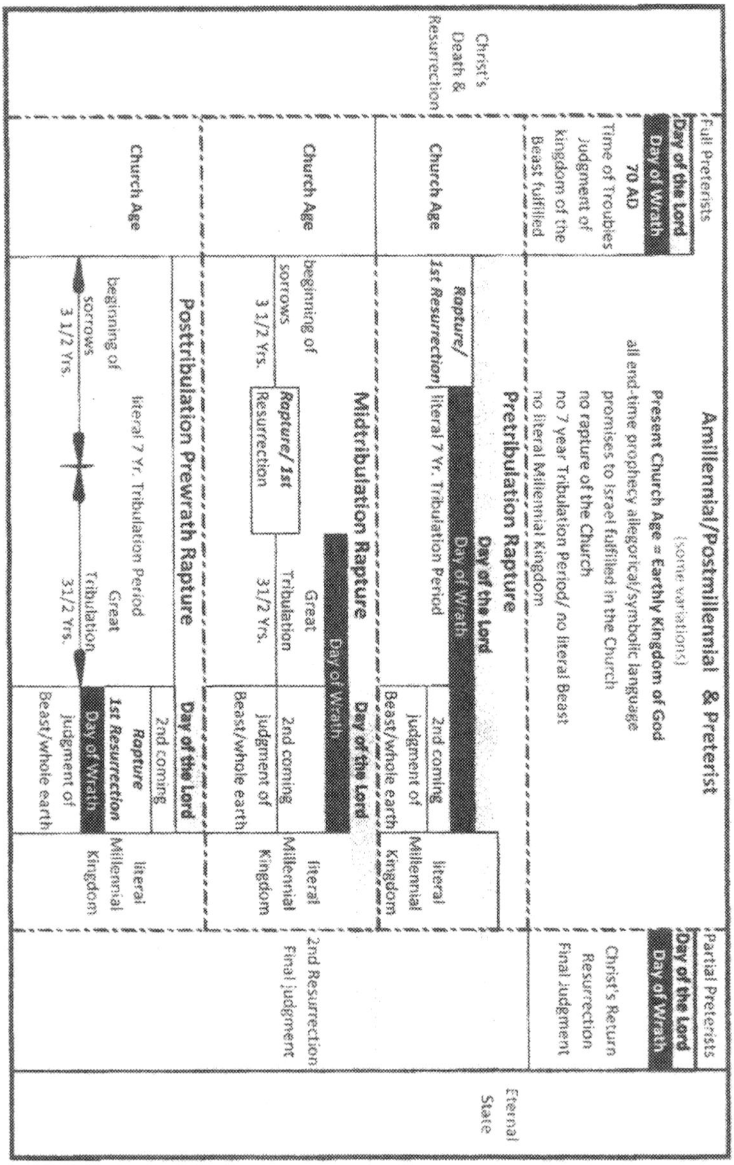
Comparison of Views - Day of Wrath
Amillennial/Postmillennial & Preterist
(some variations)
Present Church Age = Earthly Kingdom of God
all end-time prophecy allegorical/symbolic language
promises to Israel fulfilled in the Church
no rapture of the Church
no 7 year Tribulation Period/ no literal Beast
no literal Millennial Kingdom
Full Preterists
Day of the Lord
Day of Wrath
70 AD
Time of Troubles
judgment of
kingdom of the
Beast fulfilled
Partial Preterists
Day of the Lord
Day of Wrath
Christ's Return
Resurrection
Final Judgment
Christ's
Death &
Resurrection
Church Age
Pretribulation Rapture
Rapture/
1st Resurrection
literal 7 Yr. Tribulation Period
Day of the Lord
Day of Wrath
2nd coming
judgment of
Beast/whole earth
literal
Millennial
Kingdom
Church Age
Midtribulation Rapture
beginning of
sorrows
3 1/2 Yrs.
Rapture/ 1st
Resurrection
Great
Tribulation
31/2 Yrs.
Day of the Lord
Day of Wrath
2nd coming
judgment of
Beast/whole earth
literal
Millennial
Kingdom
2nd Resurrection
Final judgment
Church Age
Posttribulation Prewrath Rapture
literal 7 Yr. Tribulation Period
beginning of
sorrows
3 1/2 Yrs.
Great
Tribulation
31/2 Yrs.
Day of the Lord
2nd coming
Rapture
1st Resurrection
Day of Wrath
judgment of
Beast/whole earth
literal
Millennial
Kingdom
Eternal
State

Figure 3.1.2-1

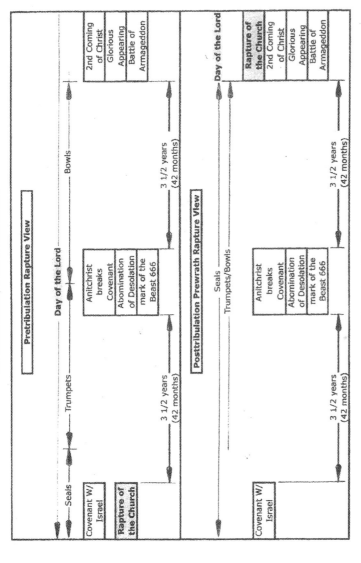

Comparison of two Views
Pretribulation vs. Posttribulation Prewrath Rapture

Figure 3.1.2-2

Here we see several statements that cry out for substantiation from Scripture. First there is the statement that this "day of the Lord will include both judgment and blessing." Dr. Constable has failed to note a critical distinction which is made in Scripture between the "day of the Lord," and the restoration of Israel. He correctly cites Zephaniah 1:14-18 as a cross reference, but throws in 3:14-15 where not only is the "day of the Lord" not mentioned, but neither is it in view at all. In the passages dealing with this day of God's judgment, the closest the prophet gets to mentioning a blessing is found in 2:3:

> *"Before the day of the Lord's anger comes upon you, seek the Lord, ... perhaps you will be hidden in the day of the Lord's anger."* *(Zeph. 2:2d-3)* [27]

In fact this warning about this day of God's judgment (which is called here "the day of the Lord") is concluded in 3:8 where it speaks of "all the earth" being "devoured by the fire of My Zeal", which clearly corresponds to other passages such as 2 Peter 3:10. The rest of Zephaniah's prophecy goes on to deal with what follows after this "day of the Lord", the restoration that will come <u>after</u> the judgment (a reoccurring pattern in the apocalyptic prophecies) - which is clearly not simultaneous with that day of judgment on the earth. This period of restoration is what John reveals in Revelation as the millennial reign of Christ on earth.[28]

Similarly, Dr. Pentecost argues that the "day of the Lord" encompasses much more than just a day of God's judgment on the earth:

> "the term *Day of the Lord*, or *that day*, is not a term which applies to a twenty-four hour period, but rather the whole program of events, including the tribulation period, the second advent program,

---

27 "Hidden" is an interesting choice of words, especially in light of what is revealed about "the Woman" in Revelation 12, and the 144,000 in Revelation 7 and 14.

28 It becomes apparent from Pentecost's remarks in his book <u>Things to Come</u> (p.230), that there is a tendency to equate "that day" or "the day" with "the day of the Lord," which may be what Dr. Constable has done in his reference to Zephaniah 3:14-15. However, such phrases are not equivalent, and the meaning of "that day" depends entirely upon the context in which the "day" intended is often designated (for example Isa. 23:15).

and the entire millennial age. It may be said to be that whole period beginning with the judgments of the seventieth week and extending through the millennial age." (Things to Come, p. 174).

Again we have to ask, where is the scriptural authority for such a strange and awkward interpretation of the word "day"? Dr. Pentecost fails to provide any or refer to any passage that would support this rather forced interpretation of the phrase. While it is true that it is not necessary to understand the word "day" to mean a twenty-four hour period of present earthly time, it clearly does not indicate a whole age of over 1000 years. When the phrase "day of the Lord" is used in other passages, which they say have already been fulfilled in history, they interpret it as a rather brief event happening suddenly at a certain point in time, never a whole era. Nor would anyone suggest that Isaiah was writing about an age which included both blessing and judgment in Isaiah 13:6 & 9, or that Joel meant anything other than a day of severe judgment in Joel 1 and 2. How inconsistent to decide that the word "day" here suddenly means a whole era, or that the expression "day of the Lord" as it appears in any Scripture passage includes a brief time of judgment but on the balance a long era of blessing and bliss. Such interpretations can only come from the reader's presuppositions, forcing certain select passages of Scripture to fit into a preconceived scenario - such as the Dispensationalist's Pretribulation Rapture theory.

When God tells us about an age, He refers to it as an age, or tells us how long it will be as in the case of the Millennium. In the case of this present period in which we are living it is called the "this age" (1 Cor. 2:6-8; Eph. 1:21) or the "time of the Gentiles," (Luke 21:24) not the "day" of the Gentiles. However, the word "day" is used many times to refer to a specific period of God's judgment which in each case was, or is to occur at a specific point in time, taking a limited period of time closer to a day than an age, or a millennium.

Most theologians and Bible commentators who subscribe to the Pre-tribulation Rapture view seem to share Drs. Constable's and Pentecost's definition of this term, "the Day of the Lord," - that it refers to a long period of time beginning with the advent of the 70th week of Daniel (for which they have adopted the term "the tribulation period"),[29] and ending after the Millennial reign of Christ on earth, after the Gog/Magog rebellion. Supposedly (according to Pentecost) others say it begins with the second coming of Christ in judgment, and ends after the Millennium.[30] Both views would include the period of 1000 years of the most blissful and perfect life on this earth that the world has ever seen since creation, as part of this "day of the Lord." And in fact, the former and seemingly more popular view would include the whole seventieth week of Daniel. For example, famous novelist Tim LaHaye et al. makes the assertion that:

> "Sometimes this phrase does refer to the glorious appearing, but on other occasions it encompasses the Rapture, the Tribulation, and the glorious appearing." [31]

Interestingly while Mr. LaHaye does admit to being inconsistent in his interpretation of this key phrase, he fails to cite any of the other passages to which he glibly refers, where the Rapture, the Tribulation (by which he means the 70th week of Daniel), and the "glorious appearing" (by which he means the second coming of Christ), are all indicated by that same phrase. Nor can they be found without heavy doses of forced interpretation, reading into the various texts certain doctrinal presuppositions. Nevertheless, he does admit that at least sometimes it is only referring to the "glorious appearing," from which we glean that it does not bother him that his approach to interpreting this phrase is quite inconsistent.

Furthermore, these interpretations being put forth by LaHaye,

---

29 This term "Tribulation Period" in itself is a misleading and confusing term in that it confuses the whole 70th week with what is referred to in Scripture as the "time of great tribulation," (also referred to as "the time of Jacob's trouble") and they are clearly not the same as there are important distinctions to be made between the two. This extra-biblical name allows them to lump together all the events of the 70th week, as if they were one entity, which they then confuse with the "day of the Lord," making the whole of Revelation chapters 4-20 fit into this one label, thereby failing to see when this day actually literally occurs in Revelation.

30 Pentecost cites Scofield as expressing this view in his notes on Jude in the Scofield Reference Bible - however his quote is not accurate as per the New Scofield Reference Edition.

31 Tim LaHaye and Thomas Ice, <u>Charting the End Times</u>, p. 108.

Constable and Pentecost, and most of those who subscribe to the Pretribulation Rapture view, feature other apparent contradictions. As has been discussed previously, they would tell us that the Millennium is God's kingdom on earth, and will be 1000 years of bliss in which the earth will be Edenic and everyone will obey and worship the one and only true God and our Lord Jesus Christ. According to them this perfect Millennial world just suddenly appears, arising out of the smoke and rubble and universal pollution that result from God's judgments on the earth (seals, trumpets, bowls and battle of HarMagedon), and is begun with a few survivors (apparently unsaved) who somehow make it through those globally cataclysmic judgments, with no explanation as to how that could be, or what kind of shape they must be in - near dead one would think. This would certainly appear to be a glaring contradiction needing a logical explanation, or at least explicit scriptural substantiation - not just assertions from men of renown (of one school of thought) that it is true.

Then, according to this same view, out of this perfect Millennial era of a restored people whose hearts have been supernaturally turned to God, comes a multitude like the sand on the seashore who really hate God, and really only want to rebel against Christ's perfect reign on earth. These unregenerate unbelievers, when the opportunity finally arises, eventually gravitate to Satan and his man Gog, and follow them in rebellion against God. All of this is supposedly happening in a brief time in the closing moments of this Millennial age. This again would seem to be a contradiction, not only logically, but with what is clearly stated in Scripture. Nowhere does Scripture tell us that there will be rebellious unbelievers in the perfect Millennial kingdom in which Christ is reigning supreme. In fact all that we are specifically told about this era is that restored and regenerated Israel will be present, with resurrected Saints reigning for a thousand years (Rev. 20:4). Even if we accept Dr. Pentecost's rather lengthy description of this Millennial kingdom, it is very difficult to explain how this rebellion happens in such a perfect setting as Scripture describes. Undeterred by such logical difficulties, Dr. Pentecost just assures us that based on "Dispensational distinctives" we just know that those living in this perfect kingdom are not all regenerate (despite what the prophets tell us about them), and their depravity causes them to rebel against God once Satan is released, and Gog shows up on the scene.

So again, according to these men we have a thousand years of Christ's perfect reign on a perfect earth (per all scriptural passages on the subject), and at the same time we have rebellion in the hearts of men which eventually leads to overt rebellion (no Scripture to support this belief) - coming from the same men who have been obeying and worshipping God throughout the whole era. This sounds a lot like a contradiction to this observer. Perhaps we need at least one clear explicit passage to support such a theory, and the strange explanations given by the men who strongly advocate this view. Just because Dispensationalists have decided that this age is not yet the eternal state in which men are perfected, but another instance of men's failure despite a perfect environment - does not make it a hermeneutic principle as they would have us believe. This is a doctrinal tenant that they have allowed to become a presupposition, from which they are launched into a pattern of circular reasoning. However, it is a tenant that is completely lacking substantiation in explicit Scripture (except as interpreted by applying their Dispensational hermeneutic - hence again, circular reasoning).

Fortunately there is no such contradiction or difficulty in the pure unadulterated explanation given by God in Scripture. In fact the simple answer is to be found exactly where we would expect it. Without fanfare it is articulated so clearly that one must stand amazed at how anyone could miss it. The answer to where these rebellious men come from is given in Revelation 20:5a - but this is the subject of another companion work, Gog/ Magog Revisited.

3.2 The "Day of the Lord" and the Creation of the New Heaven and Earth

A major source of confusion seems to be associated with the timing of the destruction of the old heavens and earth, and the creation of the new heavens and earth. If we fail to see that the judgment on the whole earth is to occur at the second coming of Christ, then we have a lot of problems. If we fail to understand that when Christ returns in judgment the world as we know it is to be destroyed by fire, as prophesied by Peter (2 Peter 3:10-12), then we have missed a critical piece of information. If we overlook the necessity that the creation of the new heaven and earth must happen after that devastating judgment is consummated, before Christ sets up His Millennial kingdom on a perfect earth (as clearly prophesied by Isaiah in Isaiah 65:17-25), then our scenario becomes nonsensical with no biblical explanation for obvious impossibilities. However, such oversights, or combination of errors, are what one must accept to subscribe to the long-age "day of the Lord" theory defined above. This subject is introduced here but discussed in considerably more detail in a companion book in this series, <u>The Millennia Kingdom and The Final Judgments on Earth And the Heavenly New Jerusalem Revisited</u> , in the chapter entitled "The Creation of the New Heavens and Earth and the Millennial Kingdom of God on earth."

Those who hold to this long-age "day of the Lord" view would argue that Revelation 21:1 is the scriptural basis for their explanation, which reads as follows:

> *"And I saw a new heaven and a new earth; for the first heaven and the first earth passed away, and there is no longer any sea." (Rev. 21:1)*

On the surface it may appear as though this is a pretty scriptural argument. But given the many other distortions and deletions of other Scripture on the subject, which is necessary to accept such an explanation, a closer examination of this verse may be called for.

Although the allusion to the destruction of heaven and earth and the creation of the new heaven and earth appearing in 21:1 follows the events of chapter 20 (the Gog/Magog rebellion and the final "Great White Throne" judgment), every Bible scholar and student of Revelation knows very well that it is absurd to suggest that the book of Revelation is to be taken in chronological order. Probably no one would argue that what is described in one chapter of the book is always or necessarily followed chronologically by what is described in another chapter. In fact John often uses the phrase "And I saw" to transition from one vision to another. Even Dr. Walvoord makes this observation when it occurs in Revelation 21:22: "The next phase of the vision is introduced with the familiar clause, 'And I saw,' indicating a new and important phase of the divine revelation" (Walvoord, p. 326). Indeed it is critical to making any sense out of this book to recognize the pattern throughout the book that there are numerous flashbacks temporally speaking, and regressions to earlier time frames chronologically. Thus it is clearly reasonable and scriptural and consistent with how we have to interpret the book to consider that perhaps the first verse of chapter 21 is simply to introduce the new subject of yet another vision.

This is not to ignore the fact that what John sees in the vision he is describing in Chapter 21 does **include** (but is not limited to) a period of time which will follow the Great White Throne judgment, and will be for many (raptured and resurrected Saints) the final eternal state. In that sense or to that degree it is chronologically sequential to the events of the preceding chapter. But to argue on this premise that the creation of the new heaven and earth must follow chronologically all the events described in previous chapters, is simply an invalid argument.

Ironically, even many of those who prescribe to the PTR eschatology do not believe that everything appearing in chapter 21 applies only to the postmillennial eternal state [32] (i.e. the period that follows the events of chapter 20) but recognize that the Millennial era is also in view in that chapter. In fact, even Dr. Pentecost seems to take what is probably the preferred position that both the eternal state and the Millennium is in view in these last two chapters. As he explains it, the eternal state is being described when "the occupants of the city are described," but the Millennial age is in view when the "occupants of the earth" are being described (Things to Come, p. 580). Hence they themselves do not really subscribe consistently to the argument that chapter 21 follows chapter 20 chronologically. How inconsistent to make such an argument for the first verse only - i.e. insisting that the destruction of the old heavens and earth and creation of the new heaven and earth must follow chronologically the Millennium and the Great White Throne judgment - and then interpret what follows as applying to the preceding Millennial era.

Perhaps Dr. Walvoord recognizes the inconsistency of such positions, and while he admits that "the book of Revelation is not written in strict chronological style" (The Revelation of Jesus Christ p. 317), nevertheless argues that "the order of Revelation beginning in chapter 19 is chronological" because "a retrogression in time would violate the structure of the last great section of the book" (p. 318). This is a classic case

---

32 Dr. Pentecost lists "Darby, Gaebelein, Grant, Ironside, Jennings, Kelly, Pettingull, Seiss, Scott, and others" as among those who hold to the view that after describing the eternal state in 21;1-8 John gives a recapitulation of the millennial age" (Things to Come, p. 563.)

of circular reasoning, or arguing from a premise. Such "retrogression" only violates Walvoord's interpretation of the structure of the book. The truth is that to ignore the retrogression in the case of the first verse necessarily involves violating what is explicitly stated in Scripture as fact - with little need for a lot of interpretation. The reason why so many scholars do resort to the "retrogressive" interpretation (which is also rather flawed logically) to which Walvoord alludes is because there is so much in these last two chapters of Revelation which apply to the Millennial era, as well as to the eternal state, and many men feel they just can't get around that fact. These problems become particularly evident when we relate these chapters in Revelation to the prophecies of Ezekiel in the last nine chapters of his book, which deal with the same future time frame.

Hence, the biggest problem with such explanations and interpretations is that they contradict what is explicitly stated in Scripture. Isaiah tells us in no uncertain terms that the millennial earth will be the newly created heaven and earth, which means that the creation of that new heavens and earth has to precede the beginning of that kingdom of God on earth:

> *"'For behold, I create new heavens and a new earth; and the former things will not be remembered or come to mind. [18] But be glad and rejoice forever in what I create; For behold, I create Jerusalem for rejoicing and her people for gladness. [19] I will also rejoice in Jerusalem and be glad in My people;... And there will no longer be heard in her the voice of weeping and the sound of crying. ... [25] The wolf and the lamb will graze together, and the lion will eat straw like the ox; and dust will be the serpent's food. They will do no evil or harm in all My holy mountain,' says the LORD." (Isaiah 65:17-25)*

It is clear that this passage in Isaiah is dealing with the Millennium. Many, if not most, Premillenarians, including Pretribulation Rapturists such as Walvoord, Pentecost, and Martin, correctly interpret this passage in Isaiah 65 as describing the Millennium. But it clearly states as explicitly as possible that the age being described begins with the creation of the "new heavens and new earth," which will include the earthly new Jerusalem. On the other hand, it is not at all clear that our text in Revelation twenty-one must be interpreted as the new heavens and new earth being created **after** the Millennium, as Dr. Martin asserts in his explanations in The

<u>Bible Knowledge Commentary</u>, or as Dr. Walvoord asserts in the passage from his book as cited above. Thus they have to resort to the following explanation:

> "...it is a common principle in prophecy to bring together events that are distantly related chronologically, such as frequent references to the first and second comings of Christ, actually separated by thousands of years (Isa. 61:1-2; cf. Luke 4:17-19). [33]

What Dr. Walvoord is doing here is applying a principle that is true, and does apply to some of the other passages cited, but does not apply to our text in Isaiah. He then also cites 2 Peter 3:10-13 as evidence of this principle, which only supports his interpretation if we make a similar logic error in understanding that passage as well - an understanding that is equally as forced and unnatural, and only dictated by his theory. However, not only do they interpret that passage as they do because of their PTR theory, but they also then try to use this convoluted interpretation of this same passage in turn to support this aspect of their theory. This latter logic error is called circular reasoning or arguing from one's premise.

Peter tells us in no uncertain terms that **we, in this church age -** not those living during the Millennium - should be "looking for and hastening" that "day of the Lord" when the judgment on the whole earth is to be executed:

> *[10]But the day of the Lord will come like a thief, in which the heavens will pass away with a roar and the elements will be destroyed with intense heat, and the earth and its works will be burned up.*
>
> *[11]Since all these things are to be destroyed in this way, what sort of people ought you to be in holy conduct and godliness, [12]**looking for and hastening the coming of the day of God, because of which the heavens will be destroyed by burning, and the elements will melt with intense heat!** [13]But according to His promise **we are looking for new heavens and a new earth**, in which righteousness dwells.*
>
> *[14]Therefore, beloved, since you look for these things, be diligent to be found by Him in peace, spotless and blameless" (2 Peter 3:10-14)*

---

33 Walvoord, p. 311.

To interpret this as referring to an event or events that will not occur until 1000 years after we have already been taken to heaven, makes no more sense than to say that this event has already happened - i.e. it is another to attempt to rewrite Scripture. God does not warn us about something, or tell the Church to be looking for and waiting expectantly for something, which He knows full well won't happen until long after she is gone - resurrected or raptured out. But that is what many of the PT Rapturists who hold to the long-age "Day of the Lord" interpretation would have us to believe.[34]

Furthermore, even if we were to take chapters 19 thru 22 of Revelation chronologically as Dr. Walvoord contends we should, it still does not support the contention that the creation of the "new heaven and earth" is to happen after the Millennium and the Great White Throne judgment of chapters 19-20. Accurate exegesis of that first verse of the 21st chapter reveals that John is **not** saying that the destruction of the former heaven and earth is occurring at that point in time, or that the new heaven and new earth is being created at that point in time. He is simply transitioning from the former vision of the Great White Throne judgment to the subject of the new heaven, new earth, and the New Jerusalem. To do so he mentions that the first heavens and first earth have passed away. It is significant that the **aorist indicative tense is used here,** which according to Greek scholars expresses **punctiliar action in past time,**[35] and he is now seeing the newly created heaven and earth. Thus he begins by providing the context for what is to follow - the discussion about the "new Jerusalem." However, he is not at this point addressing when that destruction of the heaven and earth, and the creation of the new heaven and earth are to occur. Those

---

34 Tim LaHaye is a notable exception to this tendency among PTR advocates in that he recognizes that the destruction of the heaven and earth and the creation of the new heaven and earth prophesied by Peter must happen before the Millennial Kingdom of Christ on earth commences (see The <u>Revelation Unveiled</u>).

35 A.T. Robertson renders this verb as "are passed away," but also as "went away." The KJV renders it "were passed away," and the NIV gives us "had passed away." The aorist tense would seem to indicate that at the point in time to which John is referring, the passing away of the heaven and earth had already occurred previously. As to the timing of when that event occurred, this verse gives no indication.

facts are set forth in the many other passages which have been addressed in the foregoing discussions.

Thus, to contend that "the day of the Lord" is meant to include the final postmillennial judgment of Satan and Gog and their followers, and that it is then that the whole heaven and earth is destroyed and the new heaven and earth are created, is simply to distort, or rewrite Scripture. Certainly such an interpretation could never be derived by reading, or much less studying, any or all of the passages (as cited above) describing or even mentioning this "Day of the Lord" event.

Distinctions made by PT Rapturists between a first coming of Christ only to the clouds in the air to rapture out the church (and resurrect the saved dead) before the seven year Tribulation Period begins, and a second coming all the way to the earth to judge the world and destroy it, are contrived - inventions to fit their preconceived views. It is taking the scriptural teaching that when Christ comes we will see Him coming in the clouds and meet Him in the air (the rapture), before He pours out His Divine wrath on the unsaved and rebellious kingdom of the Beast and his followers on the earth, and interjecting a Tribulation period between those two aspects of this one event. All of these are scriptural events, or aspects of the prophesied events, but the order and sequence which is so clearly spelled out in Scripture (as in Matthew 24 and 2 Thessalonians 2), are rearranged and redefined awkwardly to fit their presuppositions and preferred scenarios.

The reality is that if we put aside presuppositions such as the "Dispensational Principles" as discussed, or the preconceived theory of the Pretribulation Rapture, it becomes clear that the second coming of Christ is the scriptural "Day of the Lord," just as was believed by the early church before Origin and Augustine. In that day, when He destroys the heaven and earth, as Peter so plainly warns and Revelation describes in considerable detail, He will then recreate the new heaven and earth as one would expect, in which He sets up His kingdom on this earth. It is relatively simple, and scriptural without manipulation and modification and forced interpretations of the relevant texts, and it makes eminently more sense.

3.3 The "Day of God's Wrath"

There are a number of terms used or names given that mean essentially the same thing, including the "Day of Wrath," the "Day of God's Wrath," the "Day of the Lord's Wrath," "the outpouring of God's wrath," "the grapes of wrath," and "the wrath of the Lamb." These expressions are often if not always used to refer to "the Day of the Lord," as defined above. However, they have been redefined and used in ways that accommodate the PTR view and such revisionism is essential to the interpretations of Scripture used to support that view. In the following the expression "the Wrath of God" will be used as synonymous with the other expressions, and it's meaning in Scripture discussed.

3.3.1 The Wrath of God Defined

It is important that all of the words that were inspired by God in the writing of Scripture be accurately defined and correctly interpreted. However, none more so than the "wrath of God." In this case the Greek word is less the issue than the context in which the words are used, from which we glean what is meant by the expression used. That its use in the apocalyptic passages refers to God's judgment being meted out on Satan and a sinful world is not a controversial statement - virtually all believers agree on this point. However, how we interpret what form this wrath or judgment takes is another matter.

Perhaps it is best to begin with an attempt to define what the expression does mean as used in Scripture, and then reason together about what it manifestly does not mean. First, it is probably safe to say that God's wrath is directed toward His enemies, not His own followers and His loved ones - not saved believers. Where in Scripture is there any indication that God's own people, His elect, will have to endure His wrath being poured out on them, no matter when they are alive?

Now PTR advocates not only agree with this, but use it as an argument against the notion that God would allow His church to go through the Tribulation Period. The problem is, this argument undermines their own position, which is based on a definition of the wrath of God as being synonymous with the whole seven year Tribulation Period (dealt with in the following paragraph) – another one of those definition they have developed to fit their presuppositions discussed above. The dilemma and hence the contradiction inherent in their view is that whether or not you accept that the Church is going thru the Tribulation Period, clearly there are faithful followers of Christ who even suffer martyrdom for their faith and obedience during that period. Hence, according to their definition associated with that view, God is in fact pouring out His wrath on His own faithful followers, no matter what you choose to call them ("Church" or "Tribulation Period Saints"), during this whole period.

Aside from this rather blatant contradiction, one needs to understand what they are calling the "wrath of God." Throughout the book of Revelation we do not see God intervening to destroy or judge the Beast, or the followers of the Beast, until the very end of the period - the seventh Seal, Trumpet, and Bowl (or "Vial" per KJV) "judgments." Until that time we have natural disasters - i.e. the earthquakes and the effects of the celestial or cosmic events referred to as the "stars of the sky" which fall to earth, and the activities of evil men, the Beast and his followers, and what appears to be demonic creatures. All of these we are told are God pouring out His wrath. But that is not what Scripture says. Scripture says it is a time when Satan is unleashed, when he is pouring out his wrath, and the persecution of the Saints is the work of Satan and his minions:

> "...Woe to the earth and the sea, because the devil has come down to you, having great wrath, knowing that he has only a short time." (Revelation 12:12)

But even if we hypothetically accept for a moment the idea that it is God who is pouring out His wrath when evil men are killing massive numbers of men and torturing believers, the question is, upon whom is this wrath being poured out for this whole 7 year period ? Is it being poured out on the Beast, or those wicked men following the Beast? Again, maybe we should let Scripture speak:

> "And when the dragon saw that he was thrown down to the earth, he persecuted the woman who gave birth to the male child. [14]But the two wings of the great eagle were given to the woman, so that she could fly into the wilderness to her place, where she was nourished for a time and times and half a time, from the presence of the serpent. [15]And the serpent poured water like a river out of his mouth after the woman,

so that he might cause her to be swept away with the flood. ¹⁶But the earth helped the woman, and the earth opened its mouth and drank up the river which the dragon poured out of his mouth. ¹⁷So the dragon was enraged with the woman, and went off to make war with **the rest of her offspring, who keep the commandments of God and hold to the testimony of Jesus.***" (Revelation 12:13-17)*

It sure seems that God's Word is telling us that what is going on during this period is that Satan is going after God's people. Until the sixth Seal and the seventh Trumpet and seventh Bowl we don't see any divine intervention to deter, let alone pour out His wrath in judgment on Satan and the Beast and his followers (except perhaps for the demonic creatures of the fifth Trumpet which are released from the pit – but even they aren't being judged yet). What we do see is Satan pouring out his wrath on "the Woman," which most would probably agree refers to God's original chosen people Israel. But then we are told that He, God, supernaturally intervenes to protect them (probably only referring to saved Israel during this period, the saved "remnant," possibly the 144,000) [36] so that Satan can't even get to them. So the target then of Satan's wrath during this time becomes "the rest of her offspring, who keep the commandments of God and hold to the testimony of Jesus." If this "offspring" is not saved Israel, which is being protected by God, who is left that can be described as followers of Jesus? Obviously it would be the Saints, which we would normally refer to as "the Church."

So why would anyone say that the whole Tribulation Period is God pouring out His wrath, when the object of the wrath is God's own people, and Scripture is telling us that it is Satan who is pouring out his wrath on God's people? According to 2 Thessalonians chapter two, where these men find their key proof text (2:7), God is allowing Satan to do his evil work unrestrained for this relatively short period of time, until He (God) steps in to judge him (Satan) and all those who will be deceived by him. Hence, **God's wrath is poured out when Christ returns, and it is poured out on Satan and his followers, not on God's own people, and not for**

---

36 That this is only saved Israel, currently what we might call Messianic Jews, is deduced from the fact that we do see unsaved Israel being persecuted and killed (Revelation 11:13) during this time (mostly prophesied in Old Testament passages).

seven years. Furthermore, God is not using Satan and the Beast and the followers of the Beast to execute His judgment on Satan and the Beast and the followers of the Beast (obviously an absurd concept when clearly articulated). According to explicit Scripture it is **Christ who returns with His army of His followers and defeats Satan and his followers - this then is the outpouring of God's wrath.**

Now one might well argue that the natural disasters are God intervening supernaturally, and hence using them to pour out His wrath. However, this would be an argument from logic, their own logic, and is not so stated in Scripture. In fact if we investigate what is known about comets and meteorites, and belts of meteorites which follow the orbits of comets, there is a natural scientific explanation for all of the natural, albeit very unique and cataclysmic phenomenon described in Scripture under the sixth seal, as well as at least four of the Trumpets, and five of the Bowls. This is the subject of another book (The Seals, Trumpets and Bowls of Revelation Revisited), as are the logical connections between these various Seal, Trumpet and Bowl events. Suffice it here to say that support for the argument that the catastrophic events described in the book are all God intervening supernaturally to judge all the people on the earth, hence the whole period is the "day of God's wrath," is weak and scripturally not very supportable, nor is it entirely logical.

On the other hand, this is not to minimize the fact that such cataclysmic occurrences as even a collision with a comet, or asteroids or a belt of large meteorites, would be a part of God's predetermined judgment on the earth, and all of its inhabitants. God knew when He created the universe what all the orbits of all the celestial bodies in that universe would be, and any collisions that would eventually occur would be part of that design from the beginning. Hence, the day and the hour would have been predetermined at creation. Thus in a very real sense it would be no less divine judgment than if He just interrupted everything, all the laws that govern the universe now, and cast down a bunch of fire and brimstone, and a mountain and huge hailstones, or whatever He chose to use.

Admittedly, even if these cosmic events are to be natural disasters, they will still affect and cause suffering for God's people - hence in that sense it will be God's judgment and it will be affecting God's own people on this earth. But the affects will be indirect, much the same as they are today. Christians today suffer when they are caught in an earthquake, or a hurricane, or a tornado, or a volcano, or a flood, etc.. We don't usually ascribe such suffering to God's judgment being poured out on those people (though we have often been embarrassed by those who do make such rash statements publicly). They are considered to be tests, or trials, or just part of living in a fallen world - as Paul says, "For we know that the whole creation groans and suffers the pains of childbirth together until now" (Romans 8:22). Similarly, the natural disasters and cataclysmic cosmic events occurring during that Tribulation Period will be worse than ever before in **degree** to be sure, but not anymore judgment on God's people than it is in any other era in history.

The same promises of God's protection and preservation given to believers now will still apply at that time, as well as others that are mentioned in Revelation with regard specifically to those going through this trying time. One of those is Revelation 3:10, which when accurately translated and interpreted (discussed above) assures those who persevere in that time that God will "keep [them] in the midst of the hour of testing." In chapter 7 we see the "bond-servants of our God" - the 144,000 being sealed with a supernatural seal of protection. In chapter 9 we see mention of "the seal of God on their foreheads" clearly indicating that God's people will be protected from the suffering inflicted by the "locusts" of the fifth Trumpet. But ultimately many if not all will be allowed to suffer and die for their Master, who suffered and died for them (as did the first Apostles and multitudes down through the ages, and as are many around the world even today). To suggest that this means that this whole period is the outpouring of God's wrath, instead of Satan's working and pouring out his wrath, seems to be neither scriptural nor logical.

3.3.2 The Wrath of God versus the Tribulation Period

As has already been alluded to above, a key distinction that exists between the seven year Tribulation Period and the wrath of God, or the Day of God's wrath, has been denied or ignored. Proponents of the PTR view in fact insist that the Tribulation Period is the wrath of God, or the day of His wrath. By doing so they can argue that the Church can't possibly be present on earth during that time, because God would not pour out His wrath on His own Church. The latter is of course a true statement, backed up by Scripture (such as 1 Thessalonians 5:9). The problem is the slight of hand - treating two very different things as if they were one and the same thing, failing to make a key distinction between them, even though in fact they are clearly two very different things. It is a little bit like an intellectual "bait and switch" technique, give the listener a truth that is unquestionable, and then substituting something which sounds similar but is actually very different, acting as if the two are one and the same. [37] In fact there is no identity or even that much similarity between God's wrath, and the whole period of testing known as the Tribulation Period - the two terms are not synonymous.

Once we have accurately defined what the "Day of God's Wrath" or the wrath of God is, and what it is not, it becomes clear that we cannot call the whole 70th week of Daniel, the "Tribulation Period," the wrath of God being poured out. To do so does violence to the meaning of the term or expression, and mischaracterizes this period of God's dealings with men. And of course, it is all designed to accommodate Dispensational presuppositions and the Pretribulation Rapture view.

God has said that this period is a time of testing - testing for the whole world (Revelation 3:10). In fact He told the church in Philadelphia that it would be a time of testing for them, through which they would have to persevere but would enjoy His protection through it all. But the day of God's wrath is something quite different, and for a different purpose. It is to judge God's enemies, the enemies of Christ and His people, and to put an end to Satan and his earthly kingdom, and sin and sinners on this earth. In fact, it is a time when the present heaven and earth will be destroyed - burned up Peter tells us (2 Peter 3:10).

God is not so inefficient, or hesitant when it comes to judgment that He has to drag it out for a prolonged period of time, torturing His own

---

37 In terms of logic fallacies, this would seem to be a combination of several. Using the same term to refer to different things because the possible meanings of the word allow it, is called the error of "Equivocation." However, in this case it is more a matter of using the same word to refer to two distinctly different things - a period of testing and tribulation when Satan is unleashed being one, and divine intervention in the form of God's judgment on the earth and its inhabitants being the other. The other fallacy may be akin to the "Part -to-whole" fallacy in that the whole period is equated to the part that actually terminates and in a sense consummates the period - the outpouring of God's wrath.

loyal and obedient followers in the process, before He finally gets around to getting the job done. Once he has accomplished His other purposes for the Tribulation Period, when it is time for His wrath to be poured out, it will be swift and efficient and effective. The "Day of the Lord" as defined above, the second coming of Christ, will be the "Day of God's Wrath." It will be immediately preceded by His rescue and withdrawal ("rapture") of those still left on the earth who are His own, as well as the resurrection of those saints who had already died. They will join Him in this triumphant return, when He will pour out His wrath and His judgment on His enemies and theirs. This will happen, as is clearly indicated in Scripture, at the end of the Tribulation Period - the seventh Trumpet of Revelation chapter 11, the seventh Bowl and battle of Armageddon of chapter 16, and the coming in glory when "He treads the winepress of the fierce wrath of God Almighty" of chapter 19.

THE "IMMINENCE" ISSUE

One of the arguments most often cited to support the PT Rapture view is what is known as "the imminence of Christ's return." A superficial reading of Scripture may give one the impression that they are right. A closer look will reveal some difficult problems with how this issue is defined, how it is derived from Scripture, and how it is used to support their view of the timing of the rapture of the Church.

4.1 The "Imminence" Issue Defined

As we read the New Testament we can't help but see a sense of what seems like urgency with respect to our anticipation of Christ's coming back for His Church. One gets the impression that God wanted the readers to be constantly living expectantly with ever-present awareness and hope that Jesus could be coming soon. In fact, some passages such as those discussed in chapter one (1.1.1 & 1.1.2), could easily be understood to say that He was coming back before that first generation of believers would die (see Matthew 24:34). Hence we have a school of thought (Reformation Theology and the Preterists view) which claims to be more literal in interpreting Scripture because they take the passages that most seem to imply imminence, more literally than do the futurist - so they claim (this interpretation and view is discussed in 1.1 above and won't be repeated here). Their claim to be more literal is contradicted by the fact that they are also saying that none of the New Testament apocalyptic prophecies are to be taken literally because they were already fulfilled in A.D. 70 with the destruction of Jerusalem.

Ironically, futurist such as the PT Rapturists, who reject such interpretations that would sound the most imminent, argue nonetheless that the imminence of Christ's return taught in Scripture means that He will have to come before the Tribulation Period begins. Their claims, the logic behind them and the supposed scriptural support need to be examined and evaluated, beginning with the term itself.

The English word "imminent" is defined by Webster's New Universal Unabridged Dictionary as "appearing as if about to happen without delay; impending ..." Applied to end-times prophecy, the teaching is that Scripture portrays Christ's return to rapture out the Church as "imminent" (their word). This means that since these prophetic passages were given there was nothing that needed to happen, no prophecy that needed to be fulfilled, before Christ could return. The mantra is "Jesus could come at any time," hence the exhortation to be ready.

The argument is that in order for the return of Christ to be "imminent" it has to happen before the Tribulation Period begins, or it would not be a surprise (hence imminent), because the events of that period being fulfilled would give it away when He was coming back. Hence, part of the argument is that we can't really know or have any warning that He is coming, or it would destroy the imminence. Of course, when they say His coming is imminent, they only mean the rapture of the Church, because it would be clearly too absurd to say that His "second coming" to earth will be so imminent, since it has to happen after the 7 year Tribulation Period and anyone who knows Scripture will know the time and the season, though not the day or the hour of His return.

Perhaps the most well known advocate of the Pretribulation Rapture Theory of our day, Tim LaHaye (author of the "Left Behind" series) et. al., gives the following definition or explanation for this argument in his Popular Encyclopedia of Bible Prophecy:

"The term 'imminence' (or imminency) as applied to the rapture of the church means   that Christ may return at any moment for His church, and no biblically predicted event must necessarily precede it.... It may occur at any time and that it is the next predicted even in God's prophetic timetable. ... In addition, one cannot know precisely when an imminent event will occur. Thus one should be prepared for it to occur at any moment. *Imminent* does not mean 'soon'; the word 'soon' implies that it must occur within a short time or within a specified time, which destroys the concept of imminence. The rapture of the church has been imminent since the days of the New Testament, but it clearly was not 'soon' at that time."[38]

4.2 Problems with the Arguments based on the Imminence of Christ's Return

The problems with the Imminence argument are multi-dimensional. Beginning with the use of the term itself, then the Scripture, and of course the logic used to make this argument are all riddled with discrepancies. First the word "imminence" is not a term that is used anywhere in Scripture. It is not a word that the Holy Spirit inspired Paul, or Peter, or John, or any other writer of Scripture to use in describing Christ's return to earth. Perhaps one could hypothesize that this is just because God's vocabulary was not as vast as the wise men who coined the expression, or adopted the word upon which to build a doctrine (of course no one would say this). This in itself is not necessarily wrong, or problematic, but it does raise a flag - why do we need to resort to extra-biblical language to teach what God's Word is telling us so clearly. And when we do, how do we know for sure that what we are teaching using different (ostensibly better) words, is not introducing connotations and implications that God never intended to communicate? The truth is we don't, and this is an excellent example - a case in point if you will. Extra-biblical terminology almost always means extra-biblical concepts, teachings or doctrines, and there are many examples of this, which are beyond the scope of this study.

This is not to suggest that the whole notion of a sense of urgency, or expectant anticipation as related to our hope of Christ's return in glory and power to rescue His followers and judge the world, is invalid or unscriptural. Clearly there are a number of passages that would cause

38 LaHaye, Tim and Hindson, Ed, General Editors, The Popular Encyclopedia of Bible Prophecy, "Imminence"; Harvest House Publishers, Eugene Oregon, 2004, p. 144.

believers of almost any era since the first century church to be looking for and expecting Christ's return. And in fact several of them instruct and admonish us that we should be doing just that (such as 2 Peter 3:9-15). Hence the PT Rapturists' "imminence" argument sounds biblical and has gained widespread acceptance. And if one accepts their definition of the imminence of Christ's return, then it seems logical that the Church must be raptured out before the seven year Tribulation Period begins. The real question is, where does the Bible teach their version of the imminence of Christ's return?

Popular author Tim LaHaye, in the work cited above, gives the following references: John 14:1-3; 1 Corinthians 1:7; Titus 2:13; 1 Corinthians 16:22; 1 Thessalonians 1:9-10; 1 Thessalonians 5:4-9; James 5:8-9; 1 John 3:2-3; Revelation 22:7, 12, 20. Part of what is most interesting about this list of passages would have to be the passages LaHaye doesn't mention, which actually do address the subject matter at hand, versus the precious little real connection in the verses he cites. For someone whose claim to superiority is the more literal approach taken to interpreting Scripture, all but one (the Revelation passage) of his proof texts have little to say about the imminence of Christ's return as they stand, taken literally. Those that actually do address the issue don't really support his definition or the point he is trying to make from them. All of his arguments from these texts are based on his perception of the "implications" which he deduces from what is stated. This involves his logic about what he thinks is the meaning behind what is actually there in the text. If he is trying to prove that the rapture of the church is scriptural, he does so with a couple of them, but that is not the subject - a rapture is one thing which is not really debatable scripturally speaking, an "imminent" rapture is a different matter.

In truth these are prime examples of the kind of exegesis and reasoning that allow one to reach the conclusions he reaches. If one does not start with LaHaye's presuppositions one will not read into these texts the same implications nor reach the same conclusions. If one does not define the "Day of the Lord" and the "Wrath" of God as he does (forced and biblically unsupportable definitions, as dealt with in the preceding chapter), engaging in circular reasoning as he does, then there is no support in these passages for his interpretation regarding the imminence of the rapture, as he defines imminence.

Finally from all of the passages he mentions we do have two that actually address the subject, one in Revelation (22:7, 12, & 20) and the other in the first letter to the Thessalonians (5:4-9). In the Revelation passages we have the repeated statement "I am coming quickly." The explanation he gives for that verse, that the word "quickly" may be just as accurately understood to refer to its "suddenness" as opposed to its soonness (to happen in a short time) is probably a valid explanation (see more on this in the following section 4.4, "A Biblical and Logically Consistent Understanding of "Imminence"). However, his leap in logic from that to his conclusion that "most likely the promises relate to the rapture as imminent and ready to occur at any moment" is again telling. It is a non sequitur to say that the "sudden" nature of Christ's return means it must be imminent - with no warning that it is about to happen. Matthew 24 is all about things that are to happen suddenly, but also tells us about all the signs that people should be observing telling them that such things are about to happen - and in fact, although LaHaye denies it, Matthew 24 is describing the same thing John is writing about here in Revelation, the rapture of the church and the virtually simultaneous second coming of Christ. Ironically, his other relevant proof text in 1 Thessalonians would seem to be saying almost the opposite of the point LaHaye is making from it:

> **"But you, brethren, are not in darkness, that the day would overtake you like a thief***; ⁵for you are all sons of light and sons of day. We are neither of night nor of darkness; ⁶so then let us not sleep as others do, but let us be alert and sober. ⁷For those who sleep do their sleeping at night, and those who get drunk get drunk at night. ⁸But since we are of the day, let us be sober, having put on the breastplate of faith and love, and as a helmet, the hope of salvation. ⁹For God has not destined us for wrath, but for obtaining salvation through our Lord Jesus Christ," (1 Thessalonians 5:4-9)*

Here again we see the intrusion of the presuppositions imposing an interpretation on the text. While the passages cited, Revelation 22:7, 12 & 20, make no mention of a rapture, and certainly not one that is to occur seven years before the second coming of Christ, LaHaye tells us that this is most likely a promise about the rapture - only the rapture. Taken in context, as most commentators seem to agree, [39] it is clearly about the second coming of Christ, not some other event at another time.

The passage cited above from 1 Thessalonians, is not saying that Christ's coming will be a "'swift, unexpected appearance ...'" such that "'Jesus could come at any time'" (p. 148) - LaHaye's interpretation of it. In fact it seems to be saying that those who are children of the light will not be surprised by His coming. How else could they know except by divine revelation, seeing the signs which God warns us to look for being fulfilled?

However, he does tend to expose the soft underbelly of his position logically and scripturally by going on to mention another passage which clearly is related to the subject at hand, Revelation 16:15, "I am coming like a thief in the night" (which he also mentions in the 1 Thessalonians 5 passage). In fact, most professing believers would very likely refer to the "thief in the night" passages to support their understanding of the imminence of Christ's return (which make it curious and perhaps telling that LaHaye would leave most of them out of his list of proof texts). And indeed, those are the passages that in fact do teach us in what sense this coming is imminent. They are as follows:

> *"Therefore be on the alert, for you do not know which day your Lord is coming. [43] But be sure of this, that if the head of the house had known at what time of the night the **thief** was coming, he would have been on the alert and would not have allowed his house*

---

39 None of the commentators I have consulted explain these passages in Revelation 22 as being about the Rapture as opposed to the second coming of Christ, nor do they even suggest such a distinction, though many of them do agree with LaHaye's Pretribulation Rapture view. Even Dr. Walvoord, a most prominent advocate of that view, lists Revelation 20:20 as one of the passages that are about the second coming of Christ (see The Bible Knowledge Commentary: New Testament, "Revelation, M. The Second Coming of Christ (19:11-21))", edited by Walvoord and Zuck). The reality is that this is because there is no such distinction between the two made in Scripture, with respect to the their timing. Hence LaHaye can argue that these verses are about the rapture and be quite correct, and others can argue that it is about the second coming of Christ, which it clearly is, and also be quite correct. But when either argues that it is only about the one and not the other they have a problem scripturally speaking.

to be broken into. [44]*For this reason you also must be ready; for the Son of Man is coming at an hour when you do not think He will."* (Matthew 24:42-44)

"Now as to the times and the epochs, brethren, you have no need of anything to be written to you. For you yourselves know full well that the day of the Lord will come just **like a thief** *in the night. While they are saying, 'Peace and safety!' then destruction will come upon them suddenly like birth pangs upon a woman with child; and they shall not escape. But you, brethren,* **are not in darkness, that the day should overtake you like a thief**; *for you are all sons of light and sons of day. We are not of night nor of darkness; so then let us not sleep as others do, but let us be alert and sober."* (1 Thess. 5:2-6)

"But the day of the Lord will come **like a thief***, in which the heavens will pass away with a roar and the elements will be destroyed with intense heat, and the earth and its works will be burned up. Since all these things are to be destroyed in this way, what sort of people ought you to be in holy conduct and godliness, looking for and hastening the coming of the day of God, on account of which the heavens will be destroyed by burning, and the elements will melt with intense heat! But according to His promise we are looking for new heavens and a new earth, in which righteousness dwells."* (2 Pet. 3:10-13)

"Remember therefore what you have received and heard; and keep it, and repent. If therefore you will not wake up, I will come **like a thief***, and you will not know at what hour I will come upon you."* (Rev. 3:3)

"And I saw coming out of the mouth of the dragon and out of the mouth of the beast and out of the mouth of the false prophet, three unclean spirits like frogs; for they are spirits of demons, performing signs, which go out to the kings of the whole world, to gather them together for the war of the great day of God, the Almighty. ('Behold, I

am coming like a thief. Blessed is the one who stays awake and keeps his garments, lest he walk about naked and men see his shame.') And they gathered them together to the place which in Hebrew is called HarMagedon." (Rev. 16:13-16)

It is perhaps no mystery why Dr. LaHaye does not go to these passages primarily as his proof texts - even though they are the ones that most clearly and obviously address the subject of "imminence." Taken in context, each one of these passages is referring to the second coming of Christ in judgment. Like the passage cited above from the Olivet Discourse (Matt. 24:36-44), they are warning that those who are not watching and waiting and expecting Christ's return, will be caught unprepared when He does come. But these passages also make it clear that such should not be the case for the true believer, "the sons of light" and "sons of day." Jesus indicated clearly that He was telling us about all these signs of His coming for the express purpose that we should not be surprised and caught off guard by them:

"But when you see Jerusalem surrounded by armies, then recognize that her desolation is at hand. ²¹ Then let those who are in Judea flee to the mountains, and let those who are in the midst of the city depart, and let not those who are in the country enter the city; ²² because these are days of vengeance, in order that all things which are written may be fulfilled. ²³ Woe to those who are with child and to those who nurse babes in those days; for there will be great distress upon the land, and wrath to this people, ²⁴ and they will fall by the edge of the sword, and will be led captive into all the nations; and Jerusalem will be trampled under foot by the Gentiles until the times of the Gentiles be fulfilled.

And there will be signs in sun and moon and stars, and upon the earth dismay among nations, in perplexity at the roaring of the sea and the waves, ²⁶ men fainting from fear and the expectation of the things which are coming upon the world; for the powers of the heavens will be shaken. ²⁷ And then they will see the Son of Man coming in a cloud with power and great glory. ²⁸ But when these things begin to take place, straighten up and lift up your heads, because your redemption is drawing near.

And He told them a parable: 'Behold the fig tree and all the trees; [30] *as soon as they put forth leaves, you see it and know for yourselves that summer is now near.* [31] *Even so you, too,* **when you see these things happening, recognize that the kingdom of God is near.** [32] *Truly I say to you, this generation will not pass away until all things take place.* [33] *Heaven and earth will pass away, but My words will not pass away.'*

[34] *Be on guard, that your hearts* **may not** *be weighted down with dissipation and drunkenness and the worries of life, and that day* **come on you suddenly like a trap**; [35] *for it will come upon all those who dwell on the face of all the earth.* [36] *But keep on the alert at all times, praying in order that you may have strength to escape all these things that are about to take place and to stand before the Son of Man." (Luke 21:20-36)*

How much clearer could the message be? So much for LaHaye's "imminence." Of course his argument would be that it is the rapture of the church which is imminent, Christ's coming to "the clouds" to meet the Church in the air. But even according to his interpretation these verses are about His "second coming" which is to the earth, which he claims won't happen till seven years later. The problem is that he has already stepped into the trap of his own making. He has been unable to resist the temptation to refer to two of the "thief in the night" passages (how obvious would it be if he ignored them completely) to support his contention about the imminence of Christ's return to rapture the church. However, since according to his own line of argumentation these passages are about the second coming of Christ, this has to mean that the second coming of Christ and the rapture of the church are both parts of one virtually simultaneous event - the "Day of the Lord." But, by conveniently defining the "Day of the Lord" as including the whole Tribulation Period (as well as the ensuing thousand year reign of Christ on earth) he seems to satisfy himself that he has dodged this logically lethal bullet. Thus he seems to think he can have it both ways - the thief in the night implies the imminence of the rapture such that it is "a 'swift and unexpected appearance' … with respect to the possibility that Jesus could come at any time," but it also is referring to the second coming of Christ in judgment, which will be known and expected as to when it is to occur, which is why the second coming and the rapture can't be happening at the same time. (Huh? Is this making any sense?) [40]

Once again, the problem is that certain artifacts of the Pretribulation Rapture Theory have been introduced into the interpretation of these passages in an attempt to make the Scripture fit the proposed scenario. **There is no mention anywhere of a separate return of Christ coming <u>only to the air</u> to rapture out the church, before the Tribulation Period begins, seven years before the second coming to the earth.** This is an invention of 19th century theologians, in particular J. Darby and the Plymouth Brethren among others (some say a young girl who claimed to have a vision, others say it originated with a British Pastor named Edward Irving), and popularized by C.I. Scofield in his Scofield Reference Bible. Certainly attempts to find this concept in any earlier church teachings and writings, such as Grant Jeffrey's [41] chapter on the subject in his book <u>Apocalypse</u>, [42] are manifestly failures in trying to make the case without the same kind of circular reasoning and forced interpretations in interpreting the writings of men as they do in interpreting Scripture on the subject (no surprise here).

---

40 It is also curious that Dr. LaHaye states in this article cited above that "some posttribulationists have responded to the doctrine of imminence by claiming that all the intervening signs have already occurred, and thus Christ's return can indeed occur at any time" (p. 144). However, he has just defined his own position on "imminence" in almost the same terms: "Christ may return at any moment for His church, and no biblically predicted event must necessarily precede it." In fact, one might be hard pressed to find a posttribulationist that would take such a position, as by definition according to that view all of the events prophesied to occur during the Tribulation Period have to be fulfilled before Christ returns, even for the rapture of the Church. On the other hand, most Amillennialists claim that the events of Revelation and other apocalyptic passages have been fulfilled, which is ostensibly a major point of disagreement between Premillennialists, including Pretribulationists, and Amillennialists or Postmillennialists. LaHaye's "imminence" would make it sound like Pretribulationist agree with the Amillennialists on this key issue - which of course they do not.

41 Grant Jeffrey is a well-known author and outspoken proponent of the Pretribulation Rapture Theory. He also wrote a whole book warning us about the infamous Y2K disaster (<u>The Millennium Meltdown 2000 Y2K</u>) - which never quite materialized, as we all now know.

42 Jeffrey, Grant R., <u>Apocalypse - The Coming Judgment of the Nations</u>, Chapter 4, 1992.

In fact the early church had it right - they were looking for Christ to return to earth at which time he would rescue them and save them from the judgment, which was the wrath of God to be poured out on all the earth. It was believed to be all one "Day of the Lord" event. Then, as now, it appeared as though the time was very near. Some likely saw Diocletian, and others Nero, as possibly being the Antichrist, and they were going through a lot of persecution. Their hope was in Christ returning, to rescue them (the so-called "rapture"), and to judge their enemies. Thus there was the sense of urgency and the belief that it would happen rather suddenly. There was not however, the notion that it would have to come as a big surprise to believers who were waiting and watching. Nor is there any passage that suggests such a thing, rather the teaching is clearly to the contrary, that we should see the signs of His coming, and be prepared for it.

However, there are also some distinct differences now. Since that first church we have had the destruction of Jerusalem in AD 70, and the virtual disappearance of Israel as nation for over 1900 years. That being the case early Theologians of the 3rd and 4th century, such as Origen and St. Augustine, developed theories and ways of interpreting Scripture such that the non-existence of a Jewish state, or even as a cohesive people group in the promised land, would not be a problem with respect to end-time prophecy. The allegorical approach to interpretation paved the way for the reformers such as John Calvin, who developed the Reformed view, which is now predominantly the Preterist School of Eschatology. In all of these the non-existence of the nation Israel didn't matter, because references to Israel in end-times prophecy were interpreted allegorically, or symbolically as referring to the church - from which we get what is often referred to as "replacement theology," that the Israel of the Old Testament is replaced by the Church of the New Testament. Hence this view apparently was the dominant view for centuries, until the nation Israel appeared again on the scene.

Inspired by the late 19th century writer, Theodor Herzl (called the Father of modern Zionism and even of the modern state of Israel), Jews began returning to their homeland in what is now Israel, which was protected by the British Balfour Amendment of 1915, and recognized as a state in 1948. While the Plymouth Brethren may not have been affected by these events, the widespread acceptance of their Dispensationalists theories very likely was. Hence the dominance of the Reformed Preterits view and their "replacement theology" began to be eroded until now the Dispensationalists and the Pretribulation Rapture view may be more widely accepted, at least in Conservative Evangelical circles. For some, such as those who hold the Pre-wrath Rapture view, we have just about come full circle back to the view held by the first century church. It is also a view that is more consistent with a literal interpretation of Scripture on the subject, if we let Scripture speak for itself, and let Scripture interpret Scripture.

Another example of Dr. LaHaye's flawed logic is his insistence that for the imminence of Christ's return to have the effect of motivating believers to holy living, or of giving them hope in trying times, or a sense of joy in looking for his return, it would have to be "imminent" - "one cannot know precisely when an imminent event will occur" (LaHaye, The Popular Encyclopedia of Bible Prophecy, p. 144). This is not necessarily a logical assumption or conclusion. Knowing precisely when such an event is going to occur would be far more motivating for those living in the actual last days before it occurs, than not really knowing if or when it will happen.

For those far removed from such an event, to know that it will not happen in their lifetime, the effect would be much less, to be sure. But 2 Peter 3:10-14 (cited above) is perhaps one of the most if not the most poignant of passages on this subject of the imminence as taught in Scripture, which is understandably but noticeably missing in LaHaye's list. It is also a "thief in the night" passage, and is meant to give the reader a sense of both urgency and anticipation and to motivate them to live differently in light of Christ's return. However, it is not in LaHaye's list because it is also manifestly describing the second coming of Christ to judge the earth, not just a rapture of the Church.[43] If in fact Peter was describing an event that wasn't supposed to happen until seven years after the very Church he was trying to motivate had already been removed from the earth, what was his point in writing it - to mislead them? And if the early church understood it the way Dr LaHaye does (i.e. that it wouldn't even happen until seven years after they would be raptured out), how would this have motivated them

---

43 To his credit LaHaye is perhaps unique in that he does recognize the 2 Peter 3 passage, which describes the destruction of the heavens and earth and the creation of the new heaven and earth, must happen at the second coming of Christ, before the Millennial age begins. Others such as Walvoord see it as referring to the judgment on Gog Magog at the end of the Millennium (per their forced interpretation of Revelation 20:8).

to anything? Or for that matter, if the Church today accepts LaHaye's escapist view, how is this to motivate us? We will be long gone before any of this happens.

In fact, telling us what is going to happen, and giving us signs that we can observe happening as the day approaches, is a very effective motivator, as we see those things happening. And as we understand more of what is meant, and see more and more things happening (the latter often precedes the former), we should reasonably become more and more motivated, and more and more encouraged. At least this is the effect it is having on this observer, and I am not alone.

The fact of the matter is that God apparently wanted believers living in any era of history to be believing that Christ could be coming soon - not just suddenly, but soon, possibly in their lifetime. But He also, and perhaps even more so, wanted those who would actually be living in those last days, to have sufficient information to be able to know that He would be coming soon, not just suddenly but soon. And He has given His Holy Spirit to help us to understand what Scripture is saying about this subject, and to be able to relate them to events happening in our world. For those living in the centuries between the 1st century Church and this 21st century church, it may not have been all that important for them to understand all that was meant by Daniel's prophecies, or the New Testament eschatological prophecies. But as we enter into those last days, it becomes more and more relevant that we understand them accurately. Knowing that we won't be raptured out until Christ returns in glory, at which time He will be judging the whole earth, is in fact no less a motivator than believing that there is this theoretical seven-year gap between the two events.

Furthermore, the claim by the PT Rapturists that they really believe in this "imminence" seems conspicuously disingenuous. As Dispensationalists they interpret the passages literally which prophesy that a literal Israel will be in existence to make a covenant with her enemies. In fact they insist that it is this covenant that marks the beginning of the seven-year Tribulation Period. They believe that it is a literal temple in a literal Jerusalem, which will be desecrated by the Gentile forces of the Antichrist - Daniel's "Abomination of Desolation." Even if they say that the temple could be built in the 3½ years after the Rapture and the beginning of the Tribulation Period, they still have to have a nation Israel in Jerusalem who will make the covenant and build the temple. To say that since Christ left the first time, and promised His return, there were no prophecies that had to be fulfilled before He could fulfill that promise to begin the "Day of the Lord," is to say that either these prophecies about Israel and Jerusalem are not really prophecies that needed to be fulfilled, or to deny that they really believe in such prophecies as being literal - as their Preterist and Amillennialist opponents contend. In other words, they are again caught in another of many contradictions in the logic of their theory and what they claim to believe. Even if we accept their spurious claims that Matthew 24 was only about Israel and not the Church, and the rapture in Matthew 24 is for the "elect" of Israel only, or those saved during the Tribulation Period only, they still have to have Israel again as a nation in her land, just as we see her today. But for most of 2000 years, when they say Christ could have come with no prerequisite prophecy that needed to be fulfilled, there was no nation Israel, and Jerusalem was the home of Muslims for much of that time. No wonder the Preterists and other schools of eschatology remain unconvinced by the arguments of such futurists - they simply don't make a lot of sense, and involve glaring self-contradictions.

The truth is that LaHaye, and the other PT Rapturists know and even insist that Israel becoming a nation is not only a sure sign that we are in the end-times, but also prophecy that had to be fulfilled before Christ could return, according to Scripture. Apparently they forget this important element of their eschatological view and their interpretation of prophecy, when they at the same time state just as emphatically their doctrine of "Imminence."

Another sad reality is that while these men are claiming that their "Imminence" doctrine is necessary to motivate people to live differently, as if Jesus is coming any moment now, the exact opposite is true. People are being lulled to sleep because they are being told that none of these things prophesied in Revelation, or other end-times prophecies, are going to affect them because they are going to escape it all - they will be gone. So what does it really matter what we know or understand about end-time prophecy? Furthermore, as an observer for well over half a century of fellow believers who have been taught that Jesus could come at any moment, and they better be ready, I have seen very little evidence that this is making any difference at all in their lives. I must confess, it never had a noticeable affect on how I lived my life. On the other hand, knowing as I do now that Scripture is actually telling us that this time is coming, and it will be a time of testing and trial of our faith, even to the point of suffering and possible martyrdom, has had a very sobering affect. It changes my outlook on life, my priorities, and my choices about how I spend my time and other resources. It has motivated me to be more diligent in preparing my children for a time when things will no longer be easy as they are now, but their faith may be tested to the extreme, and their very life may be on the line. But perhaps the PT Rapturists would have me go back to the more complacent lifestyle based on the more comfortable belief that it couldn't happen to us, because we are the Church.

Even the dictionary suggests that the word "imminence" has the implication of impending doom. In that sense it is appropriate to use the word with regard to what the Scripture teaches us about the second coming of Christ as seen from the unsaved world's perspective - not so much for an escapists rapture. It is the "Day of the Lord," as seen in the preceding chapter where every passage using that term is cited - a day of judgment and destruction. However, from the perspective of the believer in Christ who is watching and waiting, to insist that Christ's return is imminent in that same sense, or even in the sense that LaHaye defines it, is completely contrary to Scripture. While we are told we will not know the exact day or hour, we are told we will have the signs that will tell us the season - like fruit on the fig tree. We are told that it will not, repeat NOT, overtake us as a thief in the night - according to the 1 Thessalonians passage cited above (which LaHaye wants to cite as Scripture supporting his "imminence" doctrine).

Certainly it is true that for the believer who knows Scripture, and in particular end-time prophecy (which are fewer and fewer in number as time goes on), seeing the events of Matthew 24 and Revelation occurring will give away the fact that Christ's second coming is getting closer and closer - so what? Is this not exactly the purpose for God revealing to us end-times prophecy? What else does the reference to "signs" of the times mean, if they are not to signify to believers that the time is drawing near? How nonsensical is it to say that God gave us all this prophecy with all these signs so that we wouldn't really know when He is coming back (referring now to the rapture) until we are gone (raptured) and it doesn't really matter to us anymore. And then as if this were not enough insult to our intelligence, to then go on to say that they are supposed to motivate us to live differently, even though we know that they won't happen until after we are long gone from the scene - could this be the wisdom of men Paul refers to in 1 Corinthians 1. Surely God is not the author of such confusion.

On the other hand, if we understand correctly what Scripture is so clearly teaching (clear if we have not been indoctrinated with presuppositions that obscure the literal natural meaning of the texts involved), it is very inspirational, encouraging and motivational to be looking for Christ's return in power and glory, to gather all His Saints from every age together (resurrection and rapture) and to lead them as a mighty army to fight the battle of Armageddon, at which time He will defeat and destroy all of our enemies, which are His enemies. At the same time, the Saints on earth are being rescued from the unrestrained wrath of Satan unleashed on this earth, and will be rewarded for their faithfulness (the Judgment Seat of Christ - an instantaneous event in God's timeless realm). The culmination will be the complete destruction of the present heaven and earth, which has largely been destroyed by the Seal, Trumpet and Bowl events of the Tribulation Period, to be replaced by a recreated new heaven and earth, the setting for the Millennial Kingdom of God on earth- a perfect, Edenic environment. What could be more exciting and motivating than that? Motivating that is to live soberly, differently than we would otherwise, as it also implies difficult times of severe testing and trial of our faith, perhaps even martyrdom - the part the PT Rapturists don't like, hence reject.

With respect to the impact of this realistic view on believers of all ages, the argument seems to be that believing that prophetic events have to be fulfilled before Christ can return, in the absence of their fulfillment people would not be at all motivated by the promise, or warning, of His coming again. In fact, going back to the first earliest church, which was the furthest removed from the fulfillment of these prophecies and promises, they were quite motivated even though they did understand that it was the second coming of Christ that was being prophesied - not a prevenient rapture, seven years earlier (which they never dreamed of). They also understood what Paul revealed in 2 Thessalonians 2, that this "Day of the Lord" would not come until after "the man of lawlessness" was revealed:

*"Now we request you, brethren, with regard to the coming of our Lord Jesus Christ and our gathering together to Him, ²that you not be quickly shaken from your composure or be disturbed either by a spirit or a message or a letter as if from us, to the effect that the day of the Lord has come. ³Let no one in any way deceive you, for **it will not come unless the apostasy comes first, and the man of lawlessness is revealed, the son of destruction,** ⁴who opposes and exalts himself above every so-called god or object of worship, so that he takes his seat in the temple of God, displaying himself as being God."* (2 Thessalonians 2:1-4)*

Hence, yes, as much as it antagonizes the PT Rapturists, one of the signs they were told to be looking for was the appearance of the Antichrist, before Christ was to come to judge that same Antichrist, and to rescue them. It is perhaps with good intentions that such men want to put a purely positive spin on the return of Christ, that it is only all good news for the believer. Escapes from reality are usually more palatable and welcome than the reality itself - hence such a message is certainly more marketable, which is important to many "Evangelicals" today. But such thinking may reflect more their fleshly material perspective, than their sincere desire to know and embrace the truth - especially if it involves both good and bad news. In fact much of the message of modern day evangelicalism is about putting a positive spin on the Gospel, such that such prominent scriptural teachings as repentance, denial of self, death of the old self, faith that produces works being essential to salvation, and perseverance in the faith being essential to ultimate salvation of the soul, are all ignored or explained away, or made out to be optional - hence cheap grace and easy believism, and once-saved-always-saved are preached instead . Eliminating a time of severe testing and trial and hence purging and cleansing of the Church before Christ returns is just another aspect of such reinvention of Christianity to suit modern evangelicals, and to make their message more acceptable, or at least less offensive, to unbelievers.

Dr. Ice, co-author with Dr LaHaye of <u>Charting the Times</u>, is able to work his magic on even this passage in 2 Thessalonians 2, and even goes beyond most of his colleagues in making it say something no unindoctrinated reader would ever understand it to say. By slightly changing the meaning of the key word "apostasy" (verse 3) to actually mean "departure," which is then interpreted as the rapture of the church, and adopting the very forced interpretation of "the Day of the Lord" held by PT Rapturists (discussed in chapter 3 above), he conveniently has the order reversed - the Antichrist doesn't appear until after the rapture of the church. [44] This is another example of the intellectually dishonest approach taken to interpreting Scripture by which such a view is maintained.

However, believers in every age who were in fact looking for the return of Christ, may have had reason to believe it could happen in their lifetime, based on the enlightenment available to them. As mentioned above, the early Church (largely "Historical Premillennialists") [45] may well have thought Diocletian or Nero was the Antichrist, and the persecution they were experiencing was what was prophesied in Revelation. Now that there is an Israel again, believers have thought that Mussolini, Hitler, various Communist dictators, and the Pope, among others were the Antichrist - hence the beginning of the Tribulation Period. More recently we have had the 10-nation European Union (which is now closer to 30 nations) perceived to be the Revived Roman Empire and the 10-horned beast of Revelation. A few today seem to be becoming more and more aware of the ways in which the rise of Islam and their power and their belief system and goals are aligned with end-times prophecy about the Beast and the kingdom of the Antichrist. As people see these signs which seem to be fulfillment of prophecy they do indeed get a sense of imminence - not

---

44 www.pre-trib.org, "The Rapture in 2 Thessalonians 2:3" by Thomas Ice. He makes the following statement: "I believe that there is a strong possibility that 2 Thessalonians 2:3 is speaking of the rapture. What do I mean? Some pretribulationists, like myself, think that the Greek noun *apostasia*, usually translated "apostasy," is a reference to the rapture and should be translated "departure." Thus, this passage would be saying that the day of the Lord will not come until the rapture comes before it. If *apostasia* is a reference to a physical departure, then 2 Thessalonians 2:3 is strong evidence for pretribulationism."

45 "Historical Premillennialism," the eschatological view of much if not most of the first few centuries of the church, held that the Antichrist first would appear on earth during the Tribulation Period, before the rapture of the Church. That would be followed by the Millennial reign of Christ on earth, and after that the final judgment of "The Great White Throne."

the imminence as LaHaye defines it, but as the dictionary defines it, "appearing as if about to happen without delay; impending ..."

After Israel was virtually annihilated it was no longer a realistic possibility biblically speaking for Christ to return at any time. However the predominant view by the fourth century became that of the allegorists, the "Amillennialists," (St. Augustine is credited with being "the Father of Amillennialism," though some Postmillennialists claim him as a forerunner of their view as well [46]) which believed the Millennial reign of Christ began at Pentecost and is not a literal 1000 years, and does not involve a literal Israel. According to this view the "Antichrist" of Scripture is symbolic, not to be taken literally as an eventual world ruler. This was the view widely held among believers through the dark ages and even persisted through the Reformation. Hence the whole concept of imminence must have been essentially abandoned, though some Amillennialists do believe that Christ is coming again to judge the earth, and some even believe in a rapture at the end of this age. But the signs of the end of the age given in passages such as Matthew 24 and most of Revelation are lost on those who hold to such a view.

However, even if the PT Rapturists were right about "imminence," or the importance of it with respect to its motivational value, in reality it wouldn't have mattered during a period when in fact significant elements of end-time prophecy had clearly not been fulfilled - such as the re-emergence of the nation of Israel in her homeland. Perhaps this, along with the apostasy of the church under Constantine's reign and the emergence of the Roman Catholic Church,[47] is why God in His sovereignty and foreknowledge allowed the church to lose their initial enlightened view and understanding of these end-time truths. Now that some of the previously unfulfilled prophetic milestones are being fulfilled (the very things PT Rapturists deny had to be fulfilled but at the same time point to as unmistakable fulfillment of prophecy indicating we are in the last times), it makes more sense for believers to be truly motivated by a sense of imminence - and some are.

But if one is to be consistent, the kind of imminence described

46 See Kenneth L Gentry Jr., Postmillennialism Made Easy, "Introduction"; 2009.

47 Premillennialism was declared to be heresy by the Catholic Church at the Council of Ephesus in AD 431.

by LaHaye would actually undermine the motivational value of such prophetic truths, as they would have no significance with respect to when Christ is coming to rapture the church, since according to that view there are no prophetic events that have to be fulfilled before Christ returns. Ironically no Premillennarian or Futurist actually believes this, not even the PT Rapturists - hence in reality even they do not really believe in the "imminence" they claim to espouse.

4.3 A Biblical and Logically Consistent Understanding of "Imminence"

There is to be sure a sense of imminence of Christ's return conveyed in Scripture. It is not the "imminence" as defined by the PTR adherents, which adds their own element of meaning to the word - that Christ's return (to rapture His Saints) must come with no prophetic events preceding it so that it could have come at any instant since His first advent and resurrection. If we stick with a dictionary definition of the word - "appearing as if about to happen without delay … impending" - then we do see this taught, or clearly implied in a number of passages. In some it is so strongly implied as to be used by the opponents of the futurist to be the proof texts in their arguments that to be true Christ must have already come back a long time ago. These are the "I am coming quickly" or "the time is near" passages.

4.3.1 The "I am coming quickly" and "the time is near" Passages

One of those, which we have addressed above, which is included in LaHaye's list (discussed in the preceding section) would be Revelation 22:6-7:

> *"And he said to me, 'These words are faithful and true; and the Lord, the God of the spirits of the prophets, sent His angel to show to His bond-servants the things which **must shortly take place**. And **behold, I am coming quickly**. Blessed is he who heeds the words of the prophecy of this book'." (Revelation 22:6-7)*

John repeats here a statement that appears in his introduction to the book of Revelation in the first verse. Referring to this revelation that he has received from God he refers to it as *"the things which must shortly take place"* (Rev. 1:1). In our text in 22:7 he adds to that: *"And behold, I am coming quickly."* Is God using John to tell us that Jesus was promising to come back soon, as in a short period of human time after His first appearance on this earth?

Here again we have a Greek word, or words, which involve a certain degree of ambiguity when we try to translate it or interpret it. The words used in Revelation 22:6 and 7, and for that matter in 1:1 and 22:20, are *tacei* and *tacu*, which are both derived from *tacus*. According to Thayer's Lexicon this word should be translated "quick, fleet, speedy". Similarly according to Bauer's Lexicon (Arndt & Gingrich), "quick, swift, speedy", indicating that when it is used in the neuter singular adverbial form (as it is in our text in 22:7) the first rendering is "quickly, at a rapid rate" and secondly "without delay, quickly, at once". The last possible rendering that they mention is "in a short time, soon".

H.K. Moulton in <u>The Analytical Greek Lexicon Revised</u> (1978 edition) specifically mentions the form of the word as it appears in 22:6 (and in 1:1 and again in 22:20), *en tacei*, rendering it "with speed, quickly, speedily; soon, shortly ... hastily, immediately". Thus most of the renderings by the Greek scholars who are only trying to get to the meaning of the word itself, is that it communicates the suddenness of something, with a secondary meaning that it sometimes communicates the imminence or "soonness" of something relative to something else. Once again we have a word that has a basic root meaning, but is used in various ways and takes on different nuances of that meaning depending upon how it is used in the context. To insist that the Greek word used here can only mean imminence as opposed to suddenness or the speed with which something prophesied will actually happen, is to simply show one's bias. Unless something in the context requires it the latter interpretation should be preferred to the former.

However, admittedly when we look at the context of both of these passages, chapter one and chapter twenty-two we do find other passages that seem to suggest that imminence or temporal proximity may be intended:

"And he said to me, 'Do not seal up the words of the prophecy of this book, for **the time is near.***'" (Revelation 1:3)*

"Blessed is he who reads and those who hear the words of the prophecy, and heed the things which are written in it; for **the time is near**.*" (Revelation 22:10)*

Here again we have a word that primarily indicates proximity, or nearness. It is often translated "at hand" in the King James Version. It seems logical that the intended meaning is that what is prophesied in this book is not that far away temporally speaking. Hence, the Preterist's say that their interpretation is more literal when they insist that it has all already been fulfilled in AD 70.

One problem with this argument is that most scholarship tends to favor a later date than AD 70 for the writing of these prophecies. Although scholars who hold to the Preterist's view of course question this, the evidence for a later date is somewhat compelling. According to one of the earliest and most recognized church historians Eusebius (AD 263-339), who twice quotes from an even earlier source, Irenaeus (2nd century Bishop of Lyon, student of Polycarp who was a disciple of the Apostle John) addressing this question of the date of the writing of the book:

> "For it was not seen a long time back, but almost in my own lifetime, at the end of Domitian's reign." (Irenaeus, Book III of <u>Heresies Answered</u>) [48]

Since we know that Domitian's reign did not end until well after AD 70 (AD 96 according to historians), it would seem to be fairly conclusive that according to a reliable witness John did not write this book at some earlier date before AD 70. Certainly if John had written before that momentous date, and had been writing about the events fulfilled at that time, Irenaeus would have known that, and would have so indicated. Certainly the burden of proof is on those who would now try to refute the testimony of witnesses so close to the time of all those events.

Another consideration is that we first see this expression used in Matthew, and Jesus said that after we see the cataclysmic sign events affecting the sun and moon and stars (also prophesied with more detail by Joel in Joel 2:28, which we see again in the sixth Seal of Rev. 6:12-17) then the time is near:

> *"even so you too, when you see all these things, recognize that He is near, right at the door." (Matt. 24:33)*

---

48 Eusebius, <u>The History of the Church from Christ to Constantine</u>, Book 5, 8.9; Penguin Books, Dorset Press, 1965, p.211.

It is hard to believe that intelligent men would try to tell us that all of these prophesied events have already taken place any time in history, let alone in that singular event in AD 70. The events that they cite as fulfillment are almost laughable unless one subscribes to their method of interpretation of the words used, which is anything but literal in any sense of the word. However, if one does subscribe to such methods then it can certainly be argued that their interpretations are as good as anyone else's, and vice versa - but then we are completely at the mercy of men to reveal to us what God meant. This is a hermeneutic that this author rejects completely as antithetical to the whole concept of divine Revelation and the enlightenment ministry of the Holy Spirit.

The very next verse, Matthew 24:34, is discussed in depth in the first chapter of this study (1.1.1) dealing with the various methods of interpretation of Scripture, because it is the most prominent passage used by the allegorical school, the Preterits, Amillennialists and Postmillennialists, to argue against the futurists who claim to be literalists:

> *"Truly I say to you, this **generation** will not pass away until all these things take place." (Matthew 24:34)*

Keeping this use of the word "generation" in context of Matthew 24, we see that Jesus goes on in the very next verse (Matt. 24:35) to mention that "heaven and earth" will pass away, which would seem to be connected with these other events being prophesied. Surely no one should be taken seriously who would suggest that this has already been fulfilled in any sense of the words used.

Once we understand that Matthew 24:34 could be just as correctly, and probably more accurately translated "this **people** shall not pass away until all these things take place" - indeed as it is most often used elsewhere, letting Scripture interpret Scripture (as is demonstrated in 1.1.1) - then the Preterists' house of cards begins to crumble. Their primary claim to being more literal than the futurists would appear itself to be an unsubstantiated claim. It would seem that this supposed fatal blow to Dispensationalism, and futurist's claims to being more consistently biblical, is itself dealt a fatal blow

Furthermore, the immediacy of the promise, or warning in this verse, Matthew 24:34, and hence its connotation of imminence, disappears like the mirage it probably is. But, the imminence of the preceding verse discussed in the preceding paragraphs, does not go away - readers are supposed to get the impression that all the events prophesied in Matthew 24 are "impending" - something they should be expecting and for which they should be preparing. So then the question remains, was God being deceptive here in implying at least the temporal proximity of these prophesied events? Or are the Preterist correct in saying they must therefore have been already fulfilled for God's Word to be true?

4.3.2 The "Thief in the Night" Passages

Again we will be best served if we let God's Word answer those questions, rather than men's logic. Letting Scripture interpret Scripture we find that indeed it is explained quite adequately in Peter's prophecy:

> *"Know this first of all, that in the last days mockers will come with their mocking, following after their own lusts, and saying, 'Where is the promise of His coming? For ever since the fathers fell asleep, all continues just as it was from the beginning of creation.' For when they maintain this, it escapes their notice that by the word of God the heavens existed long ago and the earth was formed out of water and by water, through which the world at that time was destroyed, being flooded with water. But the present heavens and earth by His word are being reserved for fire, kept for the day of judgment and destruction of ungodly men.*
>
> *But do not let this one fact escape your notice, beloved, that **with the Lord one day is as a thousand years, and a thousand years as one day.** The Lord is not slow about His promise, as some count slowness, but is patient toward you, not wishing for any to perish but for all to come to repentance. But the day of the Lord will come like a thief, in which the heavens will pass away with a roar and the elements will be destroyed with intense heat, and the earth and its works will be burned up. Since all these things are to be destroyed in this way, what sort of people ought you to be in holy conduct and godliness, looking for and hastening the coming of the day of God, on account of which the heavens will be destroyed by burning, and the elements will melt*

with intense heat! But according to His promise we are looking for new heavens and a new earth, in which righteousness dwells." (2 Pet. 3:3-12)

Here Peter acknowledges that there will be a significant enough time delay between the time the promises of Christ's return and the time of their fulfillment (including the judgment of the whole heavens and earth) that men will mock the whole idea. Their mockery will be premised upon the fact that despite the ominous threats nothing has happened for a long time. If in fact these promises were fulfilled in AD 70 as the Preterists insist, then what Peter wrote here would make little sense, and would be at best completely unnecessary (nor would it have any relevance to us today). Of course, if it was fulfilled in the relatively insignificant local event of the destruction of tiny Jerusalem, none of the prophecies are very meaningful or make much sense including Peter's words here, in that they appear to describe a global event and beyond that to a cosmically apocalyptic event. To suggest that what Peter is describing here, which matches what Jesus and several of the Old Testament prophets described, was fulfilled in the Romans destroying one small city, is on the face of it patently absurd. But to then claim the moral high ground on interpreting Scripture literally because of such an absurd obviously non-literal interpretation, as some do, is almost unbelievably self-contradictory. [49]

Peter's explanation needs no further explanation. Scripture, and particularly prophecy is written from God's perspective when it comes to time, and the timing of events. With God, who is eternal, a thousand years is like a day. This means that though a few thousand years have elapsed, from God's perspective it's only like a couple of days. Thus when He promises that these events will take place soon, He may well mean within a few thousand years. **This would be quite deceptive were it not for the fact that He has told us through Peter that this is what He means.** If anyone denies that this is what Peter means by what he clearly writes, it may be quite telling to hear what his or her explanation of this passage would be.

---

49 To suggest that it is "more literal" to take a few words like "generation" and "near" in their most narrow and unnecessarily restrictive sense, and then mutilate all the other descriptions of these end time events by dismissing them as hyperbolic language and symbolism, seems almost disingenuous, certainly inconsistent.

In this passage in 2 Peter we are also warned that this day will come **like a thief,** and it will be a day "in which the heavens will pass away with a roar and the elements will be destroyed with intense heat, and the earth and its works will be burned up" (2 Pet. 3:10). The mention here of the thief speaks of the **imminence** of this event, and ties us in with Matthew 24:43, which is clearly understood as referring to the second coming of Christ. Furthermore, Peter tells us that we - New Testament believers, "the church," - are to be "looking for and hastening the coming" of that "day of God" (2 Pet. 3:12), because associated with that day is the promised "new heavens and new earth, in which righteousness dwells" (2 Pet. 3:13).

Ironically, since this so clearly refers to the second coming of Christ to earth as being the event that is "imminent," the PT Rapturists actually deny its imminence because it refutes their theory that Christ is coming to the clouds to rapture the church seven years before this event. Their argument is that the rapture can't be occurring after the Tribulation Period at the second coming of Christ, because that would destroy the imminence of it. Hence, even though Peter tells us that it will be "like a thief in the night" - clearly intended to at least imply if not denote imminence, they tell us such an event cannot be imminent. Then they claim to be more literal - no wonder their credibility is called into question.

In fact, the explanation they give for Peter's prophecy gets even more bizarre. Many if not most [50] tell us that Peter is prophesying something that isn't going to happen until after the Millennial reign of Christ on this earth. Now if one is already committed to believing and defending their PT Rapture theory, this may not be a problem. But to an objective thinker, who is honestly and earnestly seeking the truth - this should raise some serious questions.

If this event to which Peter is referring - Christ's return in judgment and the destruction followed by the creation of the new heavens and earth - is not to happen until the end of the millennial reign of Christ on earth, why are we in this "Church age" being exhorted to be looking for it? If it is not to happen until after the 1000 year reign of Christ on earth, in what way is it to be imminent like the coming of a thief in the night. If, as they maintain, this warning in 2 Peter is referring to the judgment at the

---

50 Tim LaHaye is a notable exception as he admits that Peter is referring to a premillennial 2nd coming of Christ.

end of the Millennium, then it is not really very relevant to us today such that we would live our lives differently in anticipation of it - though that is the very point that Peter is trying to make. How confusing and sterile Scripture can become when men try to make it fit into the preconceived notions about what it can or cannot be saying.

Peter's message, or we should say God's message to us through Peter, is quite clear if we let the Scripture speak for itself. We need to be living godly lives, conducting ourselves in a holy manner, because we know that Christ is coming to get us, and to rain down fiery judgment on those who are not living in anticipation of that coming. However, it is not something to be living in dread or fear of, because it also involves the creation of that new heaven and new earth, the implementation of the Kingdom of God on earth, "the kingdom in which righteousness dwells" (2 Pet. 3:13). This "day of the Lord," and promised coming, will happen at a time when the world doesn't expect it, and they will be caught off guard as when a thief strikes (which is of course, perhaps ironically, exactly what Pretribulation Rapturists insist upon as an essential aspect of the rapture of the church - hence the doctrine of "imminence").

Furthermore, we have several other passages in which this "thief in the night" metaphor is used. LaHaye mentions the one in Revelation 16:15, which again, ironically, refutes rather than supports his explanation of "imminence" as related to the timing of the rapture. Taken in context it is obvious what is intended there:

> *"And I saw coming out of the mouth of the dragon and out of the mouth of the beast and out of the mouth of the false prophet, three unclean spirits like frogs; [14]for they are spirits of demons, performing signs, which go out to the kings of the whole world, to gather them together for the war of the great day of God, the Almighty. [15]('**Behold, I am coming like a thief. Blessed is the one who stays awake and keeps his clothes, so that he will not walk about naked and men will not see his shame.**') [16]And they gathered them together to the place which in Hebrew is called Har-Magedon." (Revelation 16:13-16)*

It is doubtful that anyone, even Dr. LaHaye, could honestly mistake this as referring to an event that is supposed to happen seven years earlier, before the Tribulation Period even begins. LaHaye refers to this "thief in the night" metaphor as communicating "imminence" - which we heartily agree it does. But it is in fact irrefutably the imminence of the second coming of Christ to earth to judge the earth, and to annihilate His enemies at the battle of Har-Magedon (also known as "Armageddon") - which LaHaye argues is not an imminent event, hence can not be when the rapture occurs. God's Word is clearly saying it is imminent, though it is occurring at the end of that Tribulation Period.

The next "thief in the night" passage, also addressed by LaHaye (also discussed in the preceding section), is in 1 Thessalonians 5:

> *¹Now as to the times and the epochs, brethren, you have no need of anything to be written to you. ²For you yourselves know full well that the **day of the Lord** will come just **like a thief in the night**. ³While they are saying, "Peace and safety!" then destruction will come upon them suddenly like labor pains upon a woman with child, and they will not escape. ⁴But you, brethren, are not in darkness, that the day would overtake you **like a thief**; ⁵for you are all sons of light and sons of day." (1 Thessalonians 5:1-5)*

Again, it is pretty difficult to mistake this for anything other than what it clearly is - the second coming of Christ in judgment: "destruction will come upon them suddenly ..." However, PT Rapturists like LaHaye introduce a very forced and scripturally unsupportable definition of the phrase "day of the Lord" (discussed in depth in Chapter 3.1 "The Definition of the "day of the Lord"), by which they deliberately obfuscate what is so clearly communicated in this, and other passages where the phrase is used. But without their pre-indoctrination the message is clear here. For those who are not "sons of light and sons of day," the second coming of Christ will catch them sleeping - totally unprepared. Even though they will have lived through all the prophesied events of the Tribulation Period, they will not recognize that Christ is coming to put an end to their disobedience. However, Paul is making it clear that such will not be the case for those who are "of the day":

> *"We are not of night nor of darkness; ⁶so then let us not sleep as others do, but let us be alert and sober. ⁷For those who sleep do their sleeping*

*at night, and those who get drunk get drunk at night. [8]But since we
are of the day, let us be sober, having put on the breastplate of faith
and love, and as a helmet, the hope of salvation. [9]For God has not
destined us for wrath, but for obtaining salvation through our Lord
Jesus Christ, [10]who died for us, so that whether we are awake or asleep,
we will live together with Him." (1 Thessalonians 5:5-10)*

Here it is as clearly stated as it can be stated. Believers who are soberly
watching and waiting for Christ's return will not be surprised by it. Hence,
the definition of "imminence" used by the PT Rapturists to support
their Pretribulation Rapture view, is again refuted by Scripture. First,
this passage clearly indicates that the believers (the Church) will be here
when the return of Christ in judgment is to happen (or, like 2 Peter 3,
this passage makes no sense at all, exhorting us to be soberly prepared for
something which none of us are ever supposed to experience). Second, just
as is indicated in Matthew 24 where the same metaphor is used (the thief),
we are specifically told it will **not** overtake us like a thief. In Matthew we
are told why we will not be surprised by it when it happens.

4.3.3 Matthew 24

*"Therefore when you see the abomination of desolation which was
spoken of through Daniel the prophet, standing in the holy place (let
the reader understand), [16]then those who are in Judea must flee to the
mountains; [17]Whoever is on the housetop must not go down to get the
things out that are in his house. [18]Whoever is in the field must not turn
back to get his cloak. [19]But woe to those who are pregnant and to those
who are nursing babies in those days! [20]But pray that your flight will
not be in the winter, or on a Sabbath. [21]For then there will be a great
tribulation, such as has not occurred since the beginning of the world
until now, nor ever will. [22]Unless those days had been cut short, no life
would have been saved; but for the sake of the elect those days will be
cut short. [23]Then if anyone says to you, 'Behold, here is the Christ,' or
'There He is,' do not believe him. [24]For false Christs and false prophets
will arise and will show great signs and wonders, so as to mislead, if
possible, even the elect. [25]Behold, I have told you in advance. [26]So if*

they say to you, 'Behold, He is in the wilderness,' do not go out, or,' Behold, He is in the inner rooms,' do not believe them. *27For just as the lightning comes from the east and flashes even to the west, so will the coming of the Son of Man be. *28Wherever the corpse is, there the vultures will gather.*29But **immediately after the tribulation of those days the sun will be darkened, and the moon will not give its light, and the stars will fall from the sky, and the powers of the heavens will be shaken**. *30And then the sign of the Son of Man will appear in the sky, and then all the tribes of the earth will mourn, and they will see the Son of Man coming on the clouds of the sky with power and great glory. *31And He will send forth His angels with a great trumpet and they will gather together His elect from the four winds, from one end of the sky to the other.

*32Now learn the parable from the fig tree: when its branch has already become tender and puts forth its leaves, you know that summer is near; *33**So, you too, when you see all these things, recognize that He is near, right at the door.***34Truly I say to you, this generation will not pass away until all these things take place. *35Heaven and earth will pass away, but My words will not pass away.

*36But of that day and hour no one knows, not even the angels of heaven, nor the Son, but the Father alone. *37For the coming of the Son of Man will be just like the days of Noah. *38For as in those days before the flood they were eating and drinking, marrying and giving in marriage, until the day that Noah entered the ark, *39and they did not understand until the flood came and took them all away; so will the coming of the Son of Man be. *40Then there will be two men in the field; one will be taken and one will be left. *41Two women will be grinding at the mill; one will be taken and one will be left.

*42Therefore be on the alert, for you do not know which day your Lord is coming. *43But be sure of this, that if the head of the house had known at what time of the night the **thief** was coming, he would have been on the alert and would not have allowed his house to be broken into. *44For this reason you also must be ready; for the Son of Man is coming at an hour when you do not think He will." (Matthew 24:15-44)

This is the same "thief in the night" event as all the others mentioned in Scripture, including that in 1 Thessalonians 5, and Revelation 16, and 1 Peter 3 addressed above. It is the "imminent" blessed hope of all those who are watching and waiting in faith for His return. It is "impending" and unexpected as an event that comes without sufficient warning, only to those who are in darkness, sons of the night, or who are not aware of the signs which He has so clearly spelled out for us. These are to be sure **prophesied events, sign events, which must happen before** that "day of the Lord," return of Christ can occur - or Scripture is not to be believed.

Now we are warned that we will not know the "day or the hour." This is however, in the same context of the passage cited above which tells us **we will know the season** - like summer coming after the winter season. This should prevent us from being deceived by the date setters - of which there have been far too many, and some exist as of the date of this writing. But that is a far cry from saying that the rapture of the church can't happen at the second coming of Christ because all of the signs given in Matthew and Revelation would give it away, and it would not be imminent. Such a contrived definition and hence doctrine of "imminence" is not coming from the Word of God.

Of course, again, false teachers are wresting the Scripture to fit their pre-conceptions. Sadly they deny that Matthew's most valuable and important prophecies are of any significance to us in the Church today, other than for informational value. By their redefinition of the "day of the Lord" (discussed previously in section 2.2.2.2) as "a literal period of time that stretches through the millennium to the new heavens and the new earth" [51] instead of the second coming of Christ, they can make any passage where that term is used refer to whatever they wish it to be, the pre-tribulation rapture, the second coming, the Millennium, or creation of the New Heaven and Earth. The exegesis seriously lacks integrity and the logic is fatally flawed, but it is a convenient interpretation when trying to make Scripture fit their view. In this case, the "day of the Lord" of Matthew

---

51 LaHaye, p. 146. His definition is right in including both the rapture and the second coming - but only because they are both part of one major event, occurring virtually simultaneously. Unfortunately, according to his view they occur seven years apart. Including the whole Millennium only makes the egregious error of their definition obvious to the intellectually honest student of Scripture.

24, referred to there as "the coming of the Son of Man," [52] is taken as the second coming, but not the rapture of the church - even though we see the most explicit description of that very rapture in this passage:

> "And then the sign of the Son of Man will appear in the sky, and then all the tribes of the earth will mourn, and they will see the Son of Man coming on the clouds of the sky with power and great glory. [31] And He will send forth His angels with a great trumpet and **they will gather together His** elect from the four winds, from one end of the sky to the other. [32] "Now learn the parable from the fig tree: when its branch has already become tender and puts forth its leaves, you know that summer is near; [33] So, you too, when you see all these things, recognize that He is near, right at the door. (Matthew 24:30-31)

Which brings us to the next invention necessary to support their theory, the specious notion that there are two comings, one to the clouds to rapture the church (and resurrect the saved dead), the second to earth to judge the earth and destroy most of it. **Nowhere does Scripture teach that Christ is coming again twice - once to the air only, the second time seven years later to the earth**. This is a relatively recent invention, reportedly of the Plymouth Brethren and John Darby of the 1850s. What we are told in Scripture is that when Christ returns He will first gather us to Himself in the air, such that we will join Him and His mighty army, all clothed in white, to participate in His victory over our enemies - Satan and all of his followers.

Ironically, if there was a passage from which you might get the idea that the rapture is an event when we go to meet him in the air before He comes to earth, it might be our text here, Matthew 24:30-31 cited above. But even the PT Rapturists concede that this is the second coming when Christ comes to earth. And indeed, it is both. However, again by simply changing the meaning of words, they deny that this passage is about the rapture of the Church at all. They argue that the "elect" in this passage is not the same as the "elect" in every other passage where the word is used, but here alone it refers to a different group, though it is not altogether

---

52 We know from the descriptions of that event here in Matthew 24 that it is the "day of the Lord" of other passages such as Joel 2 and the day of the Lord's wrath of Revelation 6 - they match in considerable detail and are surely not events that will occur more than once.

clear that they all agree on who that group is. According to some, such as Dallas Theological Seminary professor Louis A. Barbieri, it is "the gathering of those who will have become believers during the Seventieth Week of Daniel and who will have been scattered into various parts of the world because of persecution "… which "will probably also involve all Old Testament saints, whose resurrection will occur at this time, so that they may share in Messiah's kingdom." (The Bible Knowledge Commentary: New Testament, Matthew 24:27-31). According to others such as another Dallas Theological Seminary professor Dwight D. Pentecost, and Timothy LaHaye, the elect here are saved Israel, [53] though both agree that the Old Testament Saints are resurrected at this time. [54]

Another passage which has a very similar description which would certainly make one think it was about the same event is in 1 Thessalonians 4:

> [16]*For the Lord Himself will descend from heaven with a shout, with the voice of the archangel and with the trumpet of God, and the dead in Christ will rise first.* [17]*Then we who are alive and remain will be caught up together with them in the clouds to meet the Lord in the air, and so we shall always be with the Lord." (1 Thessalonians 4:16-17)*

From this the argument is made that the rapture of the church, which is what they agree is described here, cannot be happening at the second coming of Christ (what LaHaye prefers to call "the glorious appearing"). Even though Paul goes on to write about it as a day of "destruction" in the next chapter (1 Thessalonians 5:1-9), by applying their own convenient definition of "the day of the Lord," which is what Paul calls it in the following context of the 5th chapter, they contend that these are two very separate, distinct and different events.

---

53 Pentecost, Dwight D. Things to Come, p. 280. LaHaye, Tim & Hindson, Ed; The Popular Encyclopedia of Bible Prophecy, "Olivet Discourse - Who Are The Elect", p. 254.

54 It is possible that Barbieri and Pentecost and LaHaye would agree since they all see people coming to Christ during the Tribulation Period, both Jew and Gentile, and have to have them raptured out sometime. However, not all P T Rapturists agree that the Old Testament saints aren't resurrected until the end of that period, some maintaining that also happens before the Tribulation Period when they believe the rapture happens. This confusion is nothing but an artifact of their own inventions - it does not come from literal Scripture, which teach that the rapture and the resurrection of all the saved occur at the second coming of Christ - the "day of the Lord."

This is in fact a very artificial distinction which neither Paul nor any other writer of Scripture makes anywhere. There is nothing in the text to indicate that Paul is describing two different events separated by seven years and a whole Tribulation Period (70th week of Daniel). Nor is there any logical reason why they must or even should be interpreted as being different events. The fact that we are to be rescued from the earth before God pours out His judgment on it, is a no brainer. That it would happen as described, being translated to meet Him in the air as He is on His way to the earth, is what one might logically expect to happen - especially in light of the fact that it coincides with the resurrection of the saved dead, at which time we all receive our new heavenly, spiritual bodies. Since even the PT Rapturists have to concede that someone is going to be raptured out at this time, at that "day of the Lord" second coming event (they say saved Israel and the so-called "Tribulation Period Saints"), why could it not just as well be the Church? Hence another glaring inconsistency in their logic, which is all they have to support their argument for two separate events, a rapture seven years before the second coming.

When Paul assures the Thessalonians in the next chapter that "God has not destined us for wrath, but for obtaining salvation through our Lord Jesus Christ," (1 Thessalonians 5:9) taken in context, it is clearly saying that when that day of destruction comes we will not be the objects of God's wrath because that is the day of our ultimate final salvation. Several passages indicate that until that day no one's salvation will be complete - hence we all look forward to that day, even those who have preceded us in physical death. The fact that He will catch us up to meet Him in the air, before He touches down on the Mount of Olives (Zechariah 14:4) to pour out His judgment on earth, and to rescue those who recognize Him as their Lord and God (Zechariah 13), does not in any way require a seven year interval between the two aspects of this one "day of the Lord" event.[55]

Speaking of glaring discrepancies, the famous words of Shakespeare come to mind at this point - "oh what a tangled web we weave." As we have just seen, several of the prominent proponents of the PTR view,

---

55 LaHaye makes some specious arguments about the time required to rapture, resurrect, and then carry out the "Judgment Seat of Christ" events - as if God is operating in our time-space continuum, which He manifestly is not. All of these spiritual realm events will occur instantaneously - or else it will take a lot longer than 7 years to carry out in rational terms of human time.

who insist that the rapture of the church (and in fact the church) is not in Matthew 24, because it is about the second coming, then theorize that the Old Testament saints will not be resurrected until then, seven years after the rapture of the church (per their view). Yet in the 1 Thessalonians text we are clearly told that the rapture of the living will not precede the resurrection of the dead:

> [15]*For this we say to you by the word of the Lord, that we who are alive and remain until the coming of the Lord, will not precede those who have fallen asleep.* [16]*For the Lord Himself will descend from heaven with a shout, with the voice of the archangel and with the trumpet of God, and the dead in Christ will rise first. (1 Thessalonians 4:15-16)*

Once again we see the consequences of letting presuppositions interfere with a natural and literal interpretation of the text, letting Scripture interpret Scripture instead of some man-made hermeneutic such as the "dispensational distinctive." If Paul so clearly tells us that the resurrection of the deceased saints will not be preceded by the rapture of the living saints, should we not then formulate a theory which at least has them happening simultaneously? And of course if we confine ourselves to just what is explicitly stated in Scripture, without adding to or taking anything away from it, that is exactly what we get - the "day of the Lord" in which Christ returns to earth, gathering together His own who meet Him in the air, bringing them with Him in His glorious appearing to eradicate His foes, judge the earth and all of those left in it.

4.3.4 Conclusions about Biblical Imminence

It seems quite clear that God wanted the believers in that first century church to be looking for and expectantly awaiting Christ's return – they were repeatedly exhorted to do so. It also appears as though He has wanted believers of every age since then to be looking for His return, and as Peter wrote, to be living differently in light of our expectation that He is coming. Thus this element of imminence is what God intended when He gave us these promises. Even if we don't hold to the questionable teaching that "Christ is coming before the time of Great Tribulation, and could have come any time since His departure from this earth," probably virtually every generation has had reason to believe that the time was very near.

If we do take 2 Thessalonians 2 quite literally without forced manipulations to spin the meaning, and we see that the "lawless one" (commonly referred to as the "Antichrist") will be revealed before Christ returns to gather us to Himself (2 Thessalonians 2:1-4), throughout history there have been what appeared to be Antichrists, and have been believed to be the Antichrist by many. Beginning perhaps with Nero and Diocletian of the early church era, through Hitler, Mussolini, Stalin, the Catholic Pope, and more recently Khrushchev and even Saddam Hussein, to name but a few, have all been perceived to be the Antichrist by many in their day. In the last 50 years of this observers existence the sense of the imminence of Christ's return has been prevalent and prominent amongst true believers, and theories about the Beast and the Woman and who the Antichrist will be have never been in short supply. But God knew what He was doing when He inspired the writers of Scripture to portray this most momentous and climactic event as coming soon. He also was honest in explaining through Peter what He meant, and why He was portraying it this way.

Nonetheless, what all these views have in common is that they all recognize this as God's Word, divinely inspired, inerrant, accurate and reliable. And in fact much of the debate between the various factions are motivated by attempts to defend this premise, that God used John and Matthew and the other prophets and writers of Scripture to write these things, therefore they must all make sense and must all agree without contradictions. Unfortunately as men we all have severe limitations (this author being no exception), the biggest being our inability to recognize our own presuppositions and see the affects of our own biases on our reasoning processes. Intellectual honesty is not naturally adhered to by anyone, especially once one has become convinced they know the answers. It is the most natural human tendency to take a certain amount of evidence and draw conclusions, and then try to make the rest of the evidence fit those conclusions. This is probably why very well intended men, with high degrees of scholarship and sometimes impressive credentials, looking at the same set of evidence, will come to quite different conclusions.

However, to suggest that all such conclusions are going to be equally valid (a Christianized version of relativistic thinking or equivalence), is of course absurd and obviates the need for anyone even trying to draw any conclusions. There are objective rules, if you will, that must be followed in guiding our reasoning (Logic), and our interpretation of any literature, especially Scripture (they are called Hermeneutics and rules of Exegesis). To the extent that one is self-disciplined enough to follow those rules one can be guided and enlightened by the Holy Spirit to accurately handle the Word of God (2 Tim. 2:15; 1 John 2:27). However, even the Holy Spirit cannot or will not override the fleshly tendency to get caught up in a school of thought, or a doctrinal system, or a popular theory or trend, and engage in manipulating Scripture to support what one already has chosen to believe, or prefers to believe. And in fact, once one has been indoctrinated or influenced by other men whom they trust and respect, or has become excited about their own theories and ideas, it is very difficult to recognize the subjective elements of such an approach. But it is not too difficult to make the evidence that refutes those already formed conclusions, go away by rationalization. Perhaps this is why John gave us some of the promises and warnings that we see in the epilogue to this book:

> *"I testify to everyone who hears the words of the prophecy of this book: if anyone adds to them, God shall add to him the plagues which are written in this book; and if anyone takes away from the words of the book of this prophecy, God shall take away his part from the tree of life and from the holy city, which are written in this book." (Revelation 22:18-19)*

The conscious intention behind this doctrine of "imminence" may ostensibly be a good one, in that it supposedly would motivate people to live as if Christ is going to come back today and catch them doing whatever they may be doing. However, it doesn't take much observation of people who claim to hold to this view to see that it doesn't seem to be having much of the desired affect. Rather it seems to have led to a de-emphasis on the whole subject of end-time prophecy as if it is almost irrelevant to us today. Rather it seems to have resulted in a church, which for the most part is living in virtual oblivion with regard to the signs and the warnings in Scripture as to what is coming. Rather such teaching (along with other popular mainstream doctrines widely taught and believed today) has given professing Christians a false sense of security, believing that she won't have to worry about these prophesied end-time events because she will be "out-of-here" when they happen.

What could be a better setup for exactly what Jesus is warning will happen - a church that is believing that she has nothing to worry about since these end-time events won't affect her? Who is more likely to be caught by Christ coming again like a thief coming in the night, than a professing Christian who isn't paying attention to the signs Jesus and Scripture in general give us, and doesn't really care too much whether we are in the last days or not? Who is more likely to be deceived by a false prophet doing miracles, than a people who believe and trust in miracles as signs that God is at work, without knowing the truth of God's Word by which we must measure and evaluate such miracles? Who is more likely to go along with a system of government and an economic system when their very survival depends upon it, than those who have been taught that they won't even be here when the Beast (or "Antichrist") sets up his new world order? Who will be more inclined to keep on living their lives in a business as usual manner than those who are convinced that God will not allow them to go through a time of trial and tribulation such as we are clearly warned about throughout the New Testament?

Those passages which in fact teach "imminence," in the sense that it is taught at all in Scripture, are mostly referring to the suddenness with which Christ is going to come to judge the earth at His second coming. Certainly recognizing the signs of His coming spelled out in Scripture, and being ready for His return does not mean buying into the latest eschatological theory to come along. Certainly there is no admonition of Scripture to indoctrinate ourselves in a 19th and 20th century system of theology and interpretations of Scripture, any more than a 3rd or 4th century school of interpretation such as the Augustinian allegorical methodology. But it is clearly true that more of what Scripture teaches prophetically becomes clear and understandable as it is being fulfilled. However, this is strictly a case of better understanding what is written as it was written (though the full meaning was hidden to those living when it was written). It certainly does not mean that we can change the clear meaning of what is written, and introduce new concepts that are neither spelled out in Scripture, nor have they ever been taught since the first Apostle's penned it.

Clearly the "thief in the night" metaphor refers in every case to the second coming of Christ and involves an ominous warning as well as the promise of deliverance to the believer. It is imminent to the extent that it is clearly defined to be in the passages dealing with that subject (as cited above) – but not "imminent" as defined by men who have coined the term to sanctify their completely illogical and scripturally unsubstantiated doctrine, that Christ could have come part way to rapture out the church **any tim**e since His first coming. If Scripture is true at all, He could not have come when there was no Israel, and even according to the PT Rapture view, the Tribulation Period can't happen until there is an Israel and a kingdom of the Antichrist who will make the seven year covenant with Israel, according to Daniel 9:27.

Ironically**, it will be very difficult for those of such a persuasion to acknowledge the "beast" of Revelation, or the Antichrist, when in fact he does appear, because they insist that it can't happen until after the church has been raptured out** (despite the clear message of II Thessalonians 2:1-4). Thus, the emergence of those very nations as fulfillment of both Daniel and John's prophetic symbology, which should be giving us a real sense of imminence that Christ's return may be on the very near horizon, is missed completely. While insisting that "imminence" means that we must believe that He could return today (referring to the Pre-tribulation Rapture), the fact that we have <u>supposedly</u> been believing that for 2000 years does not escape the average Christian believer - hence there is in reality <u>very little sense of **urgency** among most believers</u> associated with this supposed belief in "**imminence**." It is a classic case of crying "wolf" - for about 2000 years (or at least since the mid 19th century).

On the other hand, if one begins to see those same Scriptures being fulfilled related to the Antichrist appearing on the scene, it creates a very real sense of immediacy and urgency knowing that we really are in those last days, and could actually be seven years or less away from that "great and awesome day of the Lord." It might also cause us to begin to prepare, at least spiritually and mentally, for the persecution which lies ahead of us in those days before Christ does return - something that the Pre-tribulation Rapturists completely fail to do, and in fact prevent others from doing by their assurances that "**we won't even be here**" (another little item of no mean significance which, if true, was missed or terribly underemphasized in the explicit writings of the inspired authors of Scripture).

CHAPTER 5

THE RAPTURE, THE RESURRECTION AND THE SECOND COMING OF CHRIST

Perhaps the most controversial eschatological question among conservative evangelicals who interpret scripturally literally, is the question about the timing of the rapture. Of course, this question embodies several other questions. The first question might be, what is "day of the Lord," and how does it relate to the outpouring of God's wrath, or the "day of the Lord's wrath." Another key question would be what is the "day of the Lord's wrath," versus the natural consequences of man's wickedness, the working of Satan and his followers (including demonic beings), and the natural disasters which are to occur (such as the cosmic events) - the kind of things which God has always used to try and test and judge His people?

The truth is that once we have answered these questions correctly and have recognized the correct pattern of revelation followed in the book of Revelation, the question about the nature and timing of the rapture and the resurrection of the Saints will also be answered.

5.1 The Rapture/Resurrection and The Day of the Lord or The Day of Wrath

As discussed in Chapter 3 on "The Day of the Lord," many men tell us today that this "day" is not a day at all but a period of 1007 years, beginning with the commencement of the 70th week of Daniel, and ending with a universal judgment at the close of the Millennial reign of

Christ on earth. As cited and discussed in that chapter, Dr. Pentecost and famed author Tim LaHaye, as well as other widely recognized experts on this subject, argue that the "day of the Lord" encompasses much more than just a day of God's judgment on the earth:

> "There are a number of indications that the day of the Lord will begin as soon as the rapture of the church occurs. The major events of the day of the Lord, accordingly, seem to include the Great Tribulation and God's judgment on the world preceding the second coming of Christ, as well as the judgments which attend the second coming of Christ and the entire thousand-year reign of Christ on earth." (Chafer, L.S. revised by Walvoord, J., Major Bible Themes, p. 310.)

Pretribulation Rapturists, such as those cited above, tell us that the outpouring of God's wrath includes the whole 7 years of the 70th week of Daniel, with the seven seals, trumpets, and bowls and the battle of HarMagedon. Thus they conclude that the rapture of the Church has to occur before that 70th week of Daniel begins, because we are promised that we will not have to go through that outpouring of God's wrath (1 Thess. 5:9).

However, in the foregoing chapter on the subject we have ascertained quite clearly from Scripture that the "day of the Lord" is not a long period of 1007 years, including the blissful 1000 years of Christ's reign on earth, but it is only a relatively brief period of God's judgment on the earth. We have seen clearly from explicit Scripture that neither the "day of the Lord" nor the rapture of the church will precede the opening of the sixth seal of Revelation. All we need to demonstrate conclusively that this is true are the words of Jesus according to Matthew, or Luke, or the writings of Paul (in 1 and 2 Thessalonians) which tell us clearly that the rapture does not precede the time of tribulation, and the appearance of the Antichrist (if we can take them literally and just accept what they say as authoritative - notwithstanding the fanciful explanations of scholars who must make these passages fit into their system of theology and eschatology). We have seen from several Old Testament prophecies that the "day of the Lord" does not precede but follows the cosmic sign events of Revelation six, the sixth seal (see Isa. 13:9-13; Joel 2:30-31). We have seen that both the "day of the Lord" and the rapture have to be occurring during that last half of the 70th week of Daniel since the Saints are still present but they are being persecuted by the Beast. This, Scripture tells us, will occur after the Beast breaks his covenant with Israel and begins his reign, requiring everyone to accept his mark (666) under threat of death. We have also seen that the rapture occurs simultaneous with the commencement of "the day of the Lord" (Matt. 24:29-31; 2 Thess. 2:1-2) hence cannot precede the appearance of the Beast, nor the opening of the sixth seal.

Furthermore, as mentioned previously, we have also ascertained that the believers will be taken out sometime before God's wrath is poured out on the beast and his followers. Thus it seems quite clear that the rapture must occur before, or at the very beginning of the seventh Trumpet and the seventh Bowl judgments. The question that still remains is, where between the opening of the sixth seal and the execution of the seventh trumpet/bowl judgment does this second coming of Christ occur, when this "day of the Lord" begins and the Saints are rescued from the outpouring of the grapes of God's wrath?

The truth again is that God has not forgotten to tell us when this rapture will occur. First we know from 1 Thessalonians 4:15-5:10 that it will not precede the resurrection of the saved dead. We also know that it will occur when the "day of the Lord" arrives. And in fact John has revealed to us exactly when that "day of the Lord," and that resurrection is to occur:

"And the nations were enraged, and Thy wrath came, and the time came for the dead to be judged, and the time to give their reward to Thy bond-servants the prophets and to the saints and to those who fear Thy name, the small and the great, and to destroy those who destroy the earth." (Rev. 11:18)

First we see that John is telling us that the time he is describing for us in this eleventh chapter of Revelation, is the time for the outpouring of God's wrath - the "day of the Lord's wrath," which we have shown is in fact "the day of the Lord." He then informs us that it is also the time for the "dead to be judged." This we know is **not** a reference to the day of judgment for the **unsaved** dead. Scripture is clear that such a day of judgment does not occur until "the rest of the dead come to life" (Rev.

20:5) and are then judged after the Millennial reign of Christ on this earth, at the Great White Throne judgment. The only judgment of the dead that occurs before that Millennial reign will be the "judgment seat of Christ," which is only for those who are saved. And it is in fact a judgment to determine the rewards which God's own people are to receive - which is the next thing that John mentions in that passage: "the time to give their reward to Thy bond-servants the prophets and to the saints and to those who fear Thy name, the small and the great."

If we keep this in context we see that it is describing the seventh trumpet, which John tells us is marked by Christ's coming to earth to judge and reign:

> *"And the seventh angel sounded; and there arose loud voices in heaven, saying, 'The kingdom of the world has become the kingdom of our Lord, and of His Christ; and He will reign forever and ever.' And the twenty-four elders, who sit on their thrones before God, fell on their faces and worshiped God, saying, 'We give Thee thanks, O Lord God, the Almighty, who art and who wast, because Thou hast taken Thy great power and hast begun to reign.'" (Rev. 11:15-17)*

Thus what we have is a rather clear description of exactly what we are looking for, exactly when we would expect it to occur. We have the resurrection of the saved dead and the judgment seat of Christ judgment, with the saints and the prophets receiving their reward. This is occurring just as Christ returns to judge the "nations" who are in overt rebellion against Him, and it is also the moment when Christ begins His reign on this earth. This is the "day of the Lord" as understood by the Church since its earliest beginnings (up until relatively recent times when such men as John Darby and the Plymouth Brethren introduced Dispensationalism and its stepchild, Pretribulation Rapturism). Perhaps men understood it this way because it is so clearly indicated in Scripture.

Ironically, Dr. Walvoord who many respect as the most prominent authority of our day on eschatology, a prominent advocate of the Pre-Tribulation Rapture (PTR) theory, does not even attempt to explain away this passage in his commentary on the book of Revelation (appearing in <u>The Bible Knowledge Commentary</u> which he also edited together with Dr. Zuck) nor in his book <u>The Revelation of Jesus Christ</u>. In the latter he actually gives the following argument against another commentator's explanation:

"The context seems to indicate that the resurrection of the righteous dead is especially in view rather than that of the wicked dead, who are not raised until after the millennium. The comment, which follows immediately, speaks of the reward given to the prophets who are servants of God, to saints in general, and to those who fear the name of God whether small or great. ... the verse teaches that it is a time of divine wrath, a time of resurrection of the dead and their reward..." (Walvoord, p. 185-6.)

This seems ironic because such an admission would seem to destroy his theory that the resurrection, and hence the rapture of the Church, and the judgment Seat of Christ are supposed to occur before this 70th week of Daniel (the so-called "seven year tribulation period") even begins. Here even Dr. Walvoord admits that it is occurring toward the end of that period, revealed as the seventh trumpet. PTR theologians have to ignore this obvious discrepancy, or they have to propose two resurrections, and two judgments in which the Saints are to be rewarded, one happening before the 70th week of Daniel begins, and another toward the end of that time of great tribulation. If they have the rapture occurring before the 70th week, but not all the prophets and saints are resurrected yet, then they blatantly contradict 1 Thessalonians 4:15: " For this we say to you by the word of the Lord, that we who are alive, and remain until the coming of the Lord, shall not precede those who have fallen asleep." The only way out of this dilemma would be to propose that there will be two resurrections, and two raptures and two judgments to reward believers, which probably one would think would be too foolish to propose. Unfortunately such is not the case.

Dr. Pentecost writing with regard to the resurrection in his book Things to Come, argues that Israel is not included in the first resurrection and rapture of the Church. There he makes a very valid point that Israel's resurrection will not occur until the end of the 70th week of Daniel. However, he instead proposes that there are **five stages** to God's **resurrection program** which will include **two resurrections of the saved**. The first will occur when the Church is raptured, and the second will occur toward the end of the 70th week of Daniel, which is what we see here in Revelation 11:18. [56] This second resurrection will be for Israel - the "Old Testament saints," and the so-called "tribulation period saints." [57]

However, once again Dr. Pentecost's arguments are very flawed. First, the reason why he has to have a second resurrection is only because he has assumed a "pretribulation rapture" of the Church. This is another case of circular reasoning, as in his book he is trying to prove that such a rapture is before the 70th week of Daniel begins, but throughout he assumes that to be a fact and uses it here to prove that there are two resurrections. [58] But in fact, just as there is no scriptural evidence of two such resurrections, neither is there any scriptural evidence for a resurrection or rapture before the 70th week of Daniel, unless we accept his very forced interpretations based on his doctrinal presuppositions and circular reasoning.

Furthermore, Dr. Pentecost's secondary argument for a separate rapture of the Church and Israel is as follows:

"...the resurrection of Israel does not take place at the time of the rapture because that resurrection included only those who are "in Christ" (1 Thess. 4:16) and Israel does not have that position. Further, the point is substantiated because the church is a mystery and God will complete the program for the church before resuming His program with Israel. Resurrection is a terminal event and Israel's resurrection could not come until her program were terminated." (Pentecost, p. 410).

---

56 Pentecost, p. 191.

57 Pentecost, p. 411.

58 Pentecost argues that the first resurrection when rewards are given to the Saints (New Testament church only) is in the air and the one mentioned in our text is on this earth - hence they must be two different resurrections. The problem is nothing in Scripture indicates such a distinction. True the "Judgment Seat of Christ" is in the spiritual realm, not physical and hence not of this earth. However there is no indication that the judgment and rewarding of the Saints in our text is on this earth, or that it is in any way distinct from the rapture/resurrection of the church and the "Judgment Seat of Christ." This comes from very ill-conceived logic, and his presuppositions that it is only Israel, and Israel will be rewarded during the Millennium on this earth - which are themselves fraught with difficulties when connected to this passage in Revelation 11:18, and other relevant passages of Scripture.

Thus he contends that the second coming of Christ in judgment is what he is calling a "terminal event," such that after that saved Israel will be resurrected to this earth and enter into the earthly Millennial kingdom. This he derives from what he has called "a dispensational interpretation," featuring the presupposition that the Tribulation Period is only intended as a time for judgment of Israel (at the exclusion of the church), hence the completion of God's program for Israel. The only real argument that Dr. Pentecost has to rely on to support this contention is his "dispensational principle" to which he resorts frequently, which also drives the other inventions that he has proposed. That is a principle that Dispensationalists have come up with, which they have adopted as a rule of interpretation, which apparently sounds very logical to them, but has no basis in explicit Scripture. They have decreed that the 70th week of Daniel is only about God's dealing with Israel, in particular His judgment and purification of Israel, and therefore the Church cannot be present during that period. Thus, as Pentecost asserts, God's program for the Church must be completed before resuming His program for Israel. Where is this stated in Scripture, one should ask? If such an axiomatic principle is true why hasn't God seen fit to reveal it explicitly to us?

If we examine the logic of this basic principle of that version of Dispensationalism, we find that not only is it lacking scriptural support, but neither is it so completely logical. First, if we are talking about God's program with Israel it should be remembered that by far the vast majority of Israel has already died and will not be here during that 70th week. So God is not dealing with Israel corporately and collectively, but only a few who happen to be alive on earth at that time. Thus it is misleading at best to say that God is fulfilling His promises to Israel by what He does during a brief seven-year period.

Secondly, even during the 70th week of Daniel people will have to come to Christ, and put their faith in Him, or they will have to choose to reject Him. Only on the basis of their coming to Christ will they be among the saved at the end of that period. If in fact they are so saved - and there will be both Jews and Gentiles also becoming saved on that basis during that period - what will be the difference between one who is ethnically a Jew and one who is not a Jew? The Bible seems to indicate there is no difference between the two in God's sight. And if such is the case, what will be the difference between the saved person during that period, and the saved person in any other period - such as in the present Church age? The only logical answer to both questions is **none** - which leads one to question why do we have to make a distinction between the two groups just because they are still alive when this 70th week of Daniel begins?

Although we are told that the temple will be rebuilt, and the indication is that the practices of offering sacrifices will again be going on during that era, we are not told that the message of the book of Hebrews is canceled, or the New Covenant will be replaced again with the Old Covenant, such that Jews will be saved by faith in the blood of bulls and goats instead of by faith in Jesus Christ their redeemer and Savior.

In fact there is no scriptural reason given why God would **not** be **judging and purging all of His people** on this earth, both Jew and Gentile, both Israel and the Church, during that time of the 70th week of Daniel. Rather, we have Scripture after Scripture which seems to be telling us exactly that, beginning with what Jesus said as recorded in Matthew 24 and Luke 17 and 21. Contrary to the arbitrary rule dictated to us by men who have wholeheartedly embraced this "dispensational distinctive" principle, nothing in Scripture suggests that what Jesus said in those passages was not about the Church, or for the Church. In fact in Matthew twenty-four He used the term "the elect" several times (vv. 22, 24, & 31), a term which these same theologians always interpret as referring to the Church – except in Matthew twenty-four.

Furthermore, in an effort to be consistent with that seemingly overriding principle, men such as Dr. Pentecost have to come up with such inconsistent interpretations as two raptures and two resurrections, and two returns of Christ, and justify them with reasoning that is neither logical nor scriptural. While it is true that the Old Testament prophets did not usually have the Church in view when they wrote to and about Israel, Jesus and the New Testament writers applied what they wrote to the Church where it was applicable. While it is true that God's program for Israel is not exactly the same as that for the Church, and that His promises to Israel have not all been fulfilled, it is not true that He has to take the Church out to begin fulfillment of those promises. Certainly what Pentecost asserts is not at all true, that "Israel's resurrection could not come until her program were terminated," [59] no matter when one theorizes that such a resurrection is to occur. God's program for Israel, with respect to prophecies and promises that are yet to be fulfilled, barely begins during the 70th week of Daniel, and is mostly fulfilled after that resurrection to which Pentecost subscribes. As we see from the balance of his book, even Dr. Pentecost believes that most of God's program for Israel is to be fulfilled during the Millennial reign of Christ on earth and following that time. One wonders at times if Dr. Pentecost read his own book. It seems self-contradictory to claim then that the resurrection cannot occur until God's program for Israel "were terminated" and also claim that most of those promises associated with that program don't even begin to be fulfilled until after Israel is resurrected and restored in her land.

Certainly most of the promises that are yet to be fulfilled cannot be fulfilled during the 70th week of Daniel when only a tiny fraction of all Israel will be present. Most will be fulfilled when Christ has returned and set up His kingdom on this earth, which will be an eternal kingdom. After the initial 1000 years of that eternal kingdom, God is going to bring everyone back (the second general resurrection of Rev. 20:5) and once for all either destroy the foes of Israel or cause them to repent such that they turn to Him with their whole hearts (see Ezekiel 36:24-38; 39:25-29). Then "all Israel will be saved" (Rom. 11:26), and Israel corporately and collectively will experience the fulfillment of God's forgiveness (Isaiah 40:1-2) and His many promises to her. Only then does it have any meaning to say that God is fulfilling His promises to Israel, because only then will all of Israel be present (or even a significant representation of all Israel).

However, the beginning of the fulfillment of those promises can be seen even today. Israel is being re-gathered in her land, and is again a nation. More will be fulfilled during the 70th week of Daniel as God judges for the first time all of Israel's enemies on this earth - which are also His enemies. Then He also destroys the present heaven and earth to create the new perfect heaven and earth. Following that even more will become a reality during the Millennial reign of Christ on this earth, which is an eternal kingdom. Then after that thousand-year period He brings everybody back, releases Satan and allows one last final rebellion against Him (Gog Magog), at which time they will try again to attack Israel. This

---

59 Pentecost, p. 410.

results in the complete fulfillment of the promises to Israel, and all of God's people, as He makes an end of all rebellion, and all sin and sinners, removing them from His perfect kingdom on this earth. At that time He also ends all death, and after the last and final judgment (the Great White Throne) everyone and everything realizes their eternal state.

Thus, the problem for their view is that our text specifically tells us that the "prophets and the saints" will be there. Most of Dr. Pentecost's arguments if they were true, and to the extent that they are in fact true, would only support the contention that the resurrection, and hence the rapture, is to occur at the second coming of Christ in judgment, not before this time of tribulation begins. Furthermore, the only reason for positing a second resurrection at all, even for the so-called "tribulation saints," is because one fails to realize that those tribulation saints are "the Church," and they have not been raptured out until this "day of the Lord" event when Christ comes to earth. Hence, even though the "rapture" is not explicitly mentioned in Revelation, the resurrection which must concur (albeit precede, not follow) with the rapture, which is followed by the "Judgment Seat of Christ" when the Saints are rewarded, does appear explicitly here in Revelation 11:18, as part of the seventh Trumpet event.

5.2 The "Restrainer" of 2 Thessalonians 2:6-7 Who is Taken Out of the Way

One of the most commonly cited proof texts for the Pretribulation Rapture view is as follows:

> *"⁶And you know what restrains him now, so that in his time he will be revealed. ⁷For the mystery of lawlessness is already at work; only he who now restrains will do so until he is taken out of the way." (2 Thessalonians 2:6-7)*

To the unindoctrinated it may entirely escape them that this is a description of the rapture of the church, or that the church is even mentioned in this passage. **Certainly the word church does not appear**

here, nor any of its equivalent names.[60] **Nor do**es the word rapture,[61] or any of the terms used elsewhere to refer to the rapture of the church. This is where one has to have some presuppositions and creative logic to get the right interpretation - according to the PTR advocates and theologians.

The logic is that the one doing the restraining is the Holy Spirit. Now it doesn't say the Holy Spirit, but clearly it is talking about God restraining the evil, and one can probably say that it is the form of God called the Holy Spirit who is doing the restraining. No problem, that isn't adding much to the text, and can't really be argued, nor does it need to be.

The next step in this logic chain is however a little less obvious, but does involve a truism - the Christians which make up the Church in this world are indwelt by the Holy Spirit, hence we can say that the Holy Spirit is in the church. This again is not a debatable point, except that the whole point being made here is to make the passage say that it is the presence of the Church in this world which is the "restrainer" referred to in this passage. So then, when it says that the "restrainer" is taken out of the way, it is actually saying that the church is taken out of this world - Walla, the rapture of the church.

There are just a few problems with this logic. First, God's working in this world, and especially His restraint of evil, is not only accomplished through the church, such that without her evil would not be restrained. It is not so much God that is dependent upon the church to overcome evil, but rather the church that is totally dependent upon God, yes the Spirit of God, to overcome evil.

However, let's say we accept this interpretation, that it is the presence of the Holy Spirit embodied in the church which is restraining the evil, and He takes the church out so that the restraint will be gone. Really?

---

60 Consider the irony that the PTR argument that the rapture of the church must be before the Tribulation Period described in Matthew 24 and Revelation 4-19 because the Greek word for "church" doesn't appear in those passages – but then the proof text they cite for this same pretribulation rapture makes no mention of that same word, or any other word or words that refer to the church. Is this intellectually honest?

61 Of course the English word "rapture" does not appear anywhere in the Bible, but the Greek words (such as "parousia") or phrases, such as we see in Matthew 24:30-31, 1 Thessalonians 4:16-17 and 2 Thessalonians 2:1 do denote a rapture. Nothing like any of those words appear in this PTR proof text, 2 Thessalonians 2:6-7.

Who do we find in Revelation 12:17 being attacked by Satan after God supernaturally protects "the Woman," - that group referred to there as "the rest of her children?" Who are the Saints that are persevering and are better off if they die, in 14:12-13? Who is it that the Beast of chapter 13 makes war against and overcomes in the 7th verse, or who are those who refuse to worship the image of the Beast and are killed in the 15th verse of that 13th chapter? Aren't these believers who are saved and hence indwelt by the Holy Spirit? If so, isn't the Holy Spirit present in the believers at that time - whether you arbitrarily choose to call them the "Church," or just "Tribulation Saints?" Why then is this evil being restrained by the presence of the Holy Spirit in the church now, but not being restrained by the presence of the Holy Spirit in the Saints present on earth at that time, if that is what our passage in 2 Thessalonians is talking about, or really means?

Here again, as is always the case, eisegesis (adding to the text words or meanings that aren't necessarily there) does not work very well. Men making their contributions, adding to what the word of God says, only creates distortions and confusion leading to divisions and arguments – hence the so-called controversial doctrines.

If we take the passage as it is at face value, it makes perfect sense and we don't create the nightmare of contradictions and inconsistencies in logic and interpretation, such as is created here by this very forced PTR interpretation. Unless we use the same kind of method of intellectually dishonest exegesis, the first six verses of this same chapter make such an interpretation quite impossible, as it clearly states that the coming of our Lord Jesus Christ and our gathering unto Him (the "rapture") cannot happen until the "man of Lawlessness" is revealed and sets himself up in the temple claiming to be God:

> *"¹Now we request you, brethren, with regard to **the coming of our Lord Jesus Christ and our gathering together to Him**, ²that you not be quickly shaken from your composure or be disturbed either by a spirit or a message or a letter as if from us, to the effect that the **day of the Lord** has come. ³Let no one in any way deceive you, for it **will not come unless the apostasy comes first**, and **the man of lawlessness is revealed**, the son of destruction, ⁴who opposes and*

exalts himself above every so-called god or object of worship, so that he takes his seat in the temple of God, displaying himself as being God."
(2 Thessalonians 2:1-4)

That "man of Lawlessness" is clearly the Beast of Revelation 13, often called the Antichrist. All we are actually told in the 6-7th verse is that God (or the Holy Spirit) has been and is restraining this evil one from doing what he will eventually be allowed to do. But when that restraint is "taken out of the way" he will be allowed to do all kinds of signs and miracles and will deceive all those who do not have a love for the truth. In other words, God is still sovereign, but when He allows Satan to do his thing it's going to get really ugly. There is no mention in those later verses (6-7) of the church, nor even an indirect reference to it, such as there is in the first verse - those that are gathered to Him - inarguably a clear reference to the rapture of the church.

This should be a warning to those who approach the passage with presuppositions, instead of a simple love for the truth. Furthermore, it seems doubtful that God really needs much help from human theologians in communicating what He means to say or in revealing His truth. Certainly it is not from what God has revealed and declared in Scripture that we get such nonsensical and self-contradictory scenarios, leading to all manner of dissension between believers on this issue, such as we see on this subject in the church today.

Of course the PTR advocates have their own interpretation of those first five verses, so that they don't refute their theory. They tell us it is the "day of the Lord" which comes after the appearance of the Antichrist, not the rapture. Hence, while it is fairly obvious to the unindoctrinated unbiased reader that the author is referring to the same event as "the coming of our Lord Jesus Christ and our gathering unto Him" in the first verse, and "the day of the Lord" in the second verse, they argue that he is talking about two different things. According to their interpretation he starts off in the first verse talking about the rapture, but then changes the subject in the second verse to "the day of the Lord." So it is the "day of the Lord" which can't happen until the Antichrist appears on the scene and claims to be God, but not the rapture.

Again this is an excellent example of very poor exegesis at best, forcing a very unnatural interpretation of the wording of the text to fit a preconceived theory. However, even if we accept this convoluted interpretation we still have a problem - a glaring discrepancy which seems like a contradiction in logic. If we were to accept their definition of the "day of the Lord" such that it does not include nor coincide with the rapture of the church (which is discussed above and in chapter 3), then we understand it to be referring to the whole seven year Tribulation Period, and the 1000 year Millennial age as well. So then, according to their own definition of the expression, Paul is telling us here that at least the whole seven year Tribulation Period - the "day of the Lord" - will not happen until after the Antichrist has appeared and set himself up in the temple as God. Does this make sense? According to their view the Antichrist doesn't defile the temple and set himself up as God until the midpoint of that period, which is supportable by Scripture (Daniel 9:27, 11:31, Matthew 24:15, Revelation 13). How can it be both? Can the whole Tribulation Period come after the Antichrist appears and sets himself up as God, and at the same time the Antichrist sets himself up as God at the midpoint of that period?

Here we have the results of the compounding of errors. First the day of the Lord is given a very forced, unnatural and unscriptural definition, which trips them up when they try to explain away a very clear passage that interpreted naturally and literally refutes the main tenant of their theory. The simple fact is that when we accept the clearly biblical definition of the "day of the Lord" as being that day when Christ returns - which they call "the second coming" - which includes the rapture of the church and God pouring out His wrath on Satan and all his followers, then and only then does this passage in 2 Thessalonians make perfect sense. How much better and easier it is to let the Word of God just speak for itself.

5.3 The Last Trump

The Apostle Paul tells us in 1 Corinthians that the resurrection of the saved dead will occur "at the last *trumpet*":

> *"Behold, I tell you a mystery; we shall not all sleep, but we shall all be changed, in a moment, in the twinkling of an eye, **at the last trumpet**; for the **trumpet** will sound, and the dead will be raised imperishable, and we shall be changed. For this perishable must put*

on the imperishable, and this mortal must put on immortality." (1 Cor. 15:51-53)

Many theologians deny that this "last trumpet" has any real significance other than a generalized symbolism, and would tell us that this trumpet is not related to the *trumpets* in Revelation. However, to the unindoctrinated it would certainly appear to be a clear pointer which God might be using to help us connect related Scripture which might tell us when this resurrection about which Paul writes is going to occur.

Interestingly Jesus tells us about an event which certainly sounds similar, and relates it to a similar *"trumpet"*:

*"And He will send forth His angels with a **great trumpet** and they will gather together His elect from the four winds, from one end of the sky to the other." (Matt. 24:31)*

And finally, Paul tells us again in his letter to the Thessalonians, where he clearly and inarguably is describing the rapture and the resurrection, that their arrival will be heralded by a trumpet:

*"For the Lord Himself will descend from heaven with a shout, with the voice of the archangel, and with the **trumpet** of God; and the dead in Christ shall rise first. Then we who are alive and remain shall be caught up together with them in the clouds to meet the Lord in the air, and thus we shall always be with the Lord." (1 Thess. 4:16-17)*

First the similarity between the descriptions of these three events in the three passages cited above is striking - so striking that one should require some very clear and explicit Scripture to believe that the three are not descriptions of the same events. Even though such clear and explicit Scripture is not forthcoming, and has never been produced by anyone, there are those who would deny that they are all the same event. PT Rapturists would tell us that there are two such appearances or returns of Christ. The first, they contend is a partial coming to the air, to rapture out the church before the 70th week of Daniel, which is described in the passages in 1 Corinthians and 1 Thessalonians. The passage in Matthew however, they claim, is about the "second coming" of Christ when He actually returns to the earth, after the 70th week of Daniel (the "Tribulation Period") has run its course. Instead of actual explicit Scripture cited to support this explanation appeals are made to the dispensational distinctives, or dispensational principles of interpretation, and the *a priori* assumption that there is a pretribulation rapture followed seven years later by the second coming of Christ – i.e. heavy doses of circular reasoning is required.

Once again this only illustrates the point that it is not Scripture itself that is confusing or obscure, but rather the forced interpretations of those Scriptures based on man-made systems of theology, and intellectually dishonest approaches to exegesis and interpretation. Letting Scripture speak for itself, as it is eminently capable of doing, **it is fairly clear that the second coming of Christ to earth, and the gathering of His elect (the "rapture"), and the resurrection of the saved dead, are all going to happen at virtually the same point in time, and they will be occurring** "at the last *trumpet*" exactly as Paul tells us. Furthermore, **there is no biblical reason why we should fail to connect the "last *trumpet*" which Paul wrote about, with the "seventh *trumpet*," which is also the last *trumpet*, which John tells us about in Revelation.** This is particularly true when John also tells us that this last *trumpet* is all about Christ returning to earth, the saved dead being resurrected and the Saints and Prophets receiving their rewards (Revelation 11:18 discussed above) - i.e. the "bema" judgment also known as the "judgment seat of Christ."

It would be difficult to imagine how four passages of Scripture could be tied together any clearer than what we see in these passages cited. In each we have angels, who either sound *trumpets* or their voices are like *trumpets*. In each we have Christ coming to earth [62] and gathering His elect, the saved of all ages. Where is the passage that tells us that this very unique set of events are all going to happen concurrently twice on two separate occasions? Clearly they are all the same event!

Many men have recognized this fact, and most have argued for either a Post-tribulation Rapture or a Mid-tribulation Rapture based on this truth. However, the Mid-tribulation view fails to locate accurately this seventh *trumpet*, and many who hold the Post-tribulation view fail to recognize that God is going to deliver His Church from the outpouring of His Divine wrath on the whole earth.

---

62 The 1 Corinthians 15 verses have to be kept in their context from which we see that Paul is also referring to Christ's second coming - see 1 Cor. 15:23-24.

Dr. Rosenthal, on the other hand, who was once a strong advocate of the Pretribulation Rapture theory, now sees this connection and recognizes that they are all referring to the same event, with some qualification. In his book, The Pre-Wrath Rapture of the Church, he correctly makes a strong point that the first five *seals* are not the wrath of God. [63] Rather he maintains that the outpouring of the wrath of God must begin at the opening of the seventh *seal* (last paragraph of chapter 14 of his book). However, he then goes on to conclude that the *trumpets* are the beginning of God's grapes of wrath judgments, occurring during the last 3½ years of the 70th week, and are followed temporally by the *bowls* occurring after this 3½ year period is completed. According to his diagrams the *seven trumpets* **commence** with the beginning of the "Day of the Lord," and are immediately **preceded** by the second coming of Christ, and the rapture of the Church. Thus he would group all of the seven *trumpet* judgments together and call them God's "final eschatological judgment - the last trump" (p. 193). This sounds neat, and is a tempting explanation, much closer to literal Scripture than the other explanations, but also has a number of problems.

First, the *trumpets* and *bowls* do not appear to be two completely separate sets of judgments, which would occur sequentially. Second, it is not at all clear that these *trumpet* judgments are any more divine interventions of God pouring out His wrath, than any of the other judgment events throughout the history of our world. Certainly it is not at all clear that the *trumpets* and *bowls* are any more the outpouring of God's wrath, than are the *seals*. True, the *bowls* are referred to as "*the seven bowls of God's wrath*," but the Old Testament is full of accounts of how God has used natural events and wicked men to judge people, especially Israel (as in the case of King Nebuchadnezzar and the Babylonian captivity, or deliverance from Sennacherib and the 185,000 Assyrians). However, none of these rise to the level of what is described as "*the day of the Lord*" wrath.

The cosmic events (beginning with the sixth *seal*) are cataclysmic and catastrophic events to be sure, but they are described as events of nature - celestial objects ("stars") falling to earth, causing huge earthquakes and fires and pollution. They were of course foreknown by God, planned by God,

---

63 See Dr. Rosenthal's summary at the end of chapter 12 of his book, The Prewrath Rapture of the Church.

and even scheduled by God when He created the universe, just as are all other natural disasters that have ever happened. But they **do not necessarily require immediate divine intervention** in time, space or history, to occur. The first four *trumpet* judgments would certainly appear to be associated with the natural expected results of those cosmic events - especially if they involve an encounter with asteroids, or a comet and/or a meteorite belt. The fifth *trumpet* may describe Satanic and demonic activity (one possible interpretation) in which they are given more freedom than before to inflict themselves on men (the restrainer of 2 Thess. 2:7 being taken out of the way), but it is only a matter of changes in degrees of what Satan has always been allowed to do, especially during this rise to power of the Great Dragon and the False Prophet. The sixth *trumpet*, and for that matter the sixth *bowl*, are the consequences of wicked people who organize, and follow the lead of the Beast and his prophet. None of these can truly be said to be direct acts of God's wrath being poured out - as in divine intervention. God is not into just torturing people, or playing a cat and mouse game with them. When God's intervening judgment is poured out it is intrusive, invasive, pervasive, and conclusive (as in the flood, the plagues in Egypt, or Sodom and Gomorrah, or as in the case of Ananias and Sapphira). ***Christ comes to make an end of sinful man's sinfulness and Satan's wickedness, and they are <u>the targets</u> of such wrath, <u>not the vehicles</u> for carrying it out.*** [64]

This is why the *seventh trumpet*, and the *seventh bowl*, are all clearly describing the same event - "the day of the Lord", in which we see the outpouring of God's wrath as Christ returns in power and glory to wage war against the Dragon, the Beast, the False Prophet, the Kings of the Earth, and

---

64 Nor is there literal scriptural support for the dispensationalist's contention that this period which they have dubbed "the seven year Tribulation Period," is only dealing with Israel, or is primarily about God judging and purifying Israel. While it is scripturally supportable that such judgment and purification is going on at this time, the purpose of God's judgment is unequivocally clearly and repeatedly declared throughout this book of Revelation - judgment on the Dragon (Satan), the Beast, the False Prophet, Babylon the Great Harlot, and all those who are followers of the Beast and have received his mark. The truth is that it is just as scripturally supportable if not more so, that a purification of the Church of Jesus Christ is going on during this time before God pours out His wrath, as it is that God is dealing with Israel. But the "day of the Lord" wrath is about the destruction of all of the forces of evil, not about God dealing with His own people.

all those who have chosen to follow the Beast. It is at this point that God intervenes directly and personally, and finally, in the course of human history.

A third problem with Dr. Rosenthal's explanation is that despite a convincing argument in the 14th chapter that *"the Last Trump"* of 1 Corinthians 15 is quite significant with respect to locating the Rapture and Christ's return, as mentioned above he then seemingly explains away this *last* trump as actually being the seventh *seal*, instead of the seventh *trumpet*:

> "Therefore, as the seventh seal is opened, the seven trumpet and bowl judgments progressively unfold. *They are* part of a comprehensive whole. Collectively, they are God's Day of the Lord wrath, His final eschatological judgment - *the last trump*. Since the last trump arises out of the seventh seal, and the Rapture according to Paul, occurs at the last trump: 'We shall all be changed, in a moment, in the twinkling of an eye, at the last trump' (1 Cor. 15:51-52), the Rapture must occur at the opening of the seventh seal and immediately prior to the beginning of God's wrath." (Rosenthal, pp. 193-194)

This interpretation allows him to locate the rapture before the first *trumpet*, which he considers to be part of the Day of the Lord's wrath. What he is saying here is correct as far as it goes, except that he fails to recognize that the *"last trump"* is exactly that, the **seventh *Trumpet*** - not the seventh *seal*, nor all seven *trumpets* (nor is there anything in the description of the seventh *seal* to suggest that it includes all seven *trumpets* - this is an artifact of the Pretribulation Rapture view [65]). Hence, what Paul is telling us there in 1 Corinthians 15, if

---

65 In point of fact all we are told about the seventh seal is that "there was silence in heaven for about half a hour" (Rev. 8:1). This is a strange way to describe or denote all hell breaking loose as in the trumpet and bowl judgments. Just because the description of the seven trumpets immediately follows this description of the seventh seal, does not necessarily imply that the two are connected, such that what follows is subsumed and encapsulated in what goes before - without any literary device in the text to suggest that such is the case. Such a technique of interpretation could be very useful to anybody wanting to make Scripture fit their presuppositions - from which we get all kinds of divisive doctrines and variant teachings. But it is not really intellectually honest exegesis. Ironically it causes these men to miss the more obvious connection between the sixth seal, and the rest of day of the Lord judgments, including the *trumpets* and *bowls*.

we take him literally, is that the rapture will occur with the sounding of the seventh and last *trumpet* - the final *trumpet* judgment.

This may be a relatively weak argument, if it is forced to stand alone. But it does not stand alone. As has been noted previously, we have the clear statement within the description of the seventh *trumpet* (Rev. 11:18) indicating that the first resurrection will occur at that time as will the *bema* judgment (the "judgment seat of Christ") when the raptured and resurrected saints receive their eternal rewards. Furthermore, we also have several indications in the descriptions of the first six *trumpets* and the *bowls* themselves, which strongly suggest that the rapture has not yet occurred, as addressed in the following.

5.4 Saints are Still Present During the Trumpet and Bowl Judgments

First it is worthy of our attention that we are specifically told that the fifth *trumpet* judgment is directed against only those men "who do not have the seal of God on their foreheads" (9:4b). This is a very unnecessary distinction unless it assumes that there are those present at the time whom God has sealed on their foreheads. This could be taken as referring only to the 144,000 (7:3-4 and 14:1), which are probably not raptured at all as they will be preserved in the wilderness (the Woman of Rev. 12:14) for the last 3 ½ years and will be the seed nation of Israel in the Millennial kingdom (this has to be deduced - the latter is not explicitly stated in Scripture, but is derived from a careful study of Revelation 12 and related passages). However, according to Revelation 22:4 there are also those who will be among the raptured/resurrected "bondservants" of God who will be in the heavenly kingdom (as opposed to the eternal kingdom on this earth) who are also described as having the name of God on their foreheads. Hence that description in 9:4 could also be referring to all the Saints who are God's Bondservants, which have obviously not been raptured out.

Similarly, we see that the first angel in 16:2 pours out his *bowl* into the earth and **only those "who had the mark of the beast and worshiped his image" were affected by it**. This again seems to assume that there are those present at this time that have not succumbed to the beast, and are protected by God from the effects of this plague.

Clearly we have Saints who are being persecuted and martyred by the Beast after he comes to power and implements his global economy with the mandatory "mark of the beast" (see 12:17; 13:7-10, & 15; 14:11-13). Of course we are told by men that these are converts to Christ who come to faith after the rapture of the church has already occurred – but there isn't one literal verse of Scripture which indicates such is the case. Many, such as LaHaye and Walvoord, tell us that the 144,000 will be witnessing around the world, which is an interesting theory, but again is not supported by Scripture. **From what we can determine the 144,000 witnesses are sequestered away to a safe place, where they are preserved supernaturally through this whole period. Certainly nothing in Scripture tells us that they are witnessing, and people are coming to Christ.**

Scripture does however tell us that there will be two witnesses who will have supernatural powers, which will apparently appear in the city of Jerusalem (at least at the time of their death), which will be martyred by "the beast" (Rev. 11:3-13). It is conceivable that converts will be made as a result of their ministry, especially among the Jews. We are told that some ("the rest") are terrified and give glory to the God of heaven, after these two witnesses are killed and then resurrected in view of their enemies - but this seems to coincide with the earthquake in Jerusalem which marks the second coming of Christ (the seventh *Trumpet*) - i.e. at the very end of the whole period. But even there we are not told anything about a large movement of repentance or revival. **Rather we are explicitly told repeatedly in Scripture that this whole period is a time when there will be a great falling away** ("apostasy" 2 Thess. 2:3) **when God sends a strong delusion** (2 Thess. 2:11-12). Jesus said there would be false prophets doing miracles who would "mislead, if possible, even the elect" (Matt. 24:24). Where is there any indication that people will still be coming to Christ in any significant numbers after this time of Great Tribulation (or the 70th week of Daniel) begins? [66]

---

66 It would seem reasonable to suggest that pivotal issues should be based on explicit Scripture, and not debatable interpretations that involve reading something into the text that isn't necessarily there. The claim that the church is not in Revelation (or Matthew 24) is key to the Pretribulation Rapture view. The speculative interpretation that many are coming to Christ after the Rapture of the church, which is why there are saints appearing in the Tribulation Period on this earth, is pivotal and essential to their professed fidelity to Scripture. But it is derived by inference driven by presuppositions (and circular reasoning). Is this really good exegesis, or hermeneutically sound?

In fact there really isn't any explicit indication that anyone will be coming to Christ during this time – though neither is there any explicit indication that there won't be. But **the fictitious concept that there will be a massive revival with many thousands turning to Christ during that time is simply wholesale fabrication with nothing but questionable exegesis and debatable human logic to support it**. Surely if such were to be the case God would have slipped in at least one little verse somewhere in this whole set of revelations telling us about such a momentous occurrence.[67] As it is, such a speculative approach to interpreting Scripture may make for entertaining novels and movies that might bring in a lot of money to the producers and marketers, but would also allow anyone to come up with all kinds of competing theories and novels and movies.

Again, aside from Dispensational Principles, which are little more than doctrinal presuppositions (some of which are indeed biblically supportable – but none of those require a pretribulation rapture) there is no scriptural reason to suggest that the saints being martyred in this time of tribulation, even during the last 3 ½ years of the great tribulation, are anything other than the church.

5.5 The "thief in the night" Warning

A clear indication that the rapture has not occurred before the sixth and seventh *bowls* have been poured out is the 15th verse of the 16th chapter:

> *"Behold, I am coming like a thief. Blessed is the one who stays awake and keeps his garments, lest he walk about naked and men see his shame." (Revelation. 16:15)*

If we accept the "verbal plenary inspiration" of Scripture, we must realize that the Holy Spirit inspired John to insert this here. If God put this here at this point in the text, He must have had a good reason for doing

---

67 This is not to ignore Matthew 24:14, but rather to argue that *"the end"* mentioned there is not a reference to some revival occurring during the 70th Week of Daniel, or the time of great tribulation, but is the end as described in Revelation 20, after the general resurrection of the unsaved dead (20:5), and just before the Great White Throne judgment - the actual end before the eternal state begins. It is the time of world-wide evangelism described in Isaiah 66:15-24.

so. If the rapture has already occurred before the first six bowl judgments have transpired, then this fifteenth verse of the sixteenth chapter is very obtusely inserted into the flow of the text, and clearly doesn't fit or belong there. However, it seems more likely that we again have another key to understanding the timing of events in Revelation.

Clearly this phrase, "**coming like a thief**," is the expression that is used repeatedly throughout the New Testament to refer to the **imminence** of Christ's coming, and the coming of the Day of the Lord (see Matt. 24:42-43, Luke 12:39-40, 2 Pet. 3:10; 1 Thess. 5:2,4, and Rev. 3:3). In most of these cases it is readily understood as **an admonition to believers to be watching and waiting for this return - clearly assuming that they will be there when this day happens**. Hence, as is usually understood by the average lay reader, these are references to the **rapture**, as well as "the day of the Lord" and the beginning of God's judgment on the earth.

Even Dr. Walvoord acknowledges that in this case the saints referred to "are evidently those still on earth who have been able to escape martyrdom even though remaining true to their Lord." [68] However, in order to hold to his preconceptions associated with the PTR view, Dr. Walvoord has to interpret this as not referring to the rapture,[69] but rather just the end of the so-called "tribulation period," and the saints present are those whom he contends are saved during that seven year period. Thus, as the PTR view requires them to do, theologians of this school either have to ignore the thorny question of what happens to these Saints who endure and survive this tribulation period, or they have to accept one or the other of two possibilities. Either there is a second rapture (which Dr. Walvoord certainly seems to be suggesting, but avoids articulating clearly) - for which one would be hard pressed to find scriptural support - or they have these tribulation Saints going through the outpouring of God's wrath - which

---

68 Walvoord, The Revelation of Jesus Christ, p. 238.

69 Dr. Walvoord avoids the use of the word "rapture" here, despite his references to the other passages, such as Matt. 24:43 and 1 Thess. 5:2, where taken in context the rapture is clearly in view as well as "*the day of the Lord*" (1 Thess. 5:2). However, instead of mentioning the rapture he uses the expression "the second coming of Christ" which fits better with their PTR view as they make a distinction between the rapture, and the so-called "second coming" - a distinction which is certainly not derived from, nor consistent with the relevant passages mentioned.

is clearly contradictory to Scripture, as well as their own logic (one of their arguments for a "pre-tribulation rapture" is that God would not allow His Church to go through this time of His judgment on earth).

Scripture is neither confused nor confusing on this point. The passages cited above are consistent and make perfect sense when understood to be referring to the return of Christ both to rapture out His Church, and to execute judgment. **It only becomes consistent and all fits together, including the placement of this "thief in the night" passage of Rev. 16:15 appearing where it does, when we realize and accept the fact that this rapture and the return of Christ (the so-called "second coming") occur simultaneously, after the sixth bowl judgment is already happening, and concurrent with the beginning of the seventh bowl judgment, which is also the seventh trumpet.**

5.6 The judgment on Jerusalem

Finally we have the problem of the **judgment on Jerusalem** (Revelation 11:13) occurring after the two witnesses have been martyred, and concurrent with their resurrection. Both of these events occur **after** the sixth trumpet, but seemingly concurrent with the seventh trumpet judgment (11:15-19). Since we already have ascertained that these witnesses must appear during the last 3½ years of this 70th week of Daniel, then we know that this martyrdom and resurrection of the two witnesses, described in 11:7-13, must be occurring at the end of this seven-year period. If we do not recognize this subsequent earthquake in Jerusalem as being virtually concurrent with (perhaps immediately preceding) the earthquake and hailstorm of the seventh trumpet (and hence the seventh bowl), then when does it occur, and what is the sequence and timing of these events? Surely none of them are occurring any very significant length of time after this seven-year period has elapsed. If they are occurring after these two witnesses are killed and resurrected, then they must be happening rapidly immediately thereafter to be within that seven-year time span. The most that Scripture allows anywhere is an extra 75 days, which is mentioned by Daniel without explanation as to what, it signifies.[70]

Dr. Rosenthal contends that it is during the first 30 days following the

---

70 Daniel does make an allusion to a period of 1335 days in Daniel 12:12, versus the 1260, saying that those who *"attain"* to the end of that time are *"blessed."*

end of this seven year period (1260 days) that the bowl judgments occur. This comes from the 1290 days mentioned in Daniel 12:11. However, he is also presuming that the seven bowl judgments are all included in the seventh *trumpet* judgment (the same explanation given by such noted PT Rapturists as Dr. Walvoord), for which he fails to make a convincing case. This would allow for a 30 day lapse between the judgment on Jerusalem and the judgments on the rest of the world, but fails to provide any rationale as to why there needs to be such a lapse, or what requires that they be two entirely separate events. Nor is it explained why the resurrection and rapture of the two witnesses should occur as an isolated event, separate from the resurrection and rapture of all Saints (though the latter is not mentioned in that same immediate text - which allows perhaps for an argument from silence to be made).

Some will argue that there are clearly two separate earthquakes in Jerusalem, this one in 11:13 and another in 16:19, and they are clearly separate events in that in the one in chapter eleven only one tenth of the city is affected, and in chapter sixteen it is one third. Obviously it is true that they are not the same event being described but two separate earthquakes. However, a close look at the passage in chapter sixteen would lead one to understand that the "great city" mentioned there is a reference to Babylon, not Jerusalem (Babylon is referred to as the "great city" more often than is Jerusalem - in fact no less than five times in chapter seventeen and eighteen). Thus the account in chapter eleven would be the only description of what happens to literal Jerusalem during the seventh *trumpet* and *bowl* judgments, as the earthquake of chapter 16 is not about Jerusalem, but Babylon. If this is not referring to the final judgment (seventh *trumpet* and seventh *bowl*) on Jerusalem, then we have no account of what happens there during those judgments. This would seem to be a strange oversight given the centrality of Jerusalem to all that is transpiring during this time. But in fact, this is the account right where it should be, closely associated with the seventh *trumpet*, and the picture is complete, just as one would expect from God.

If one can put aside all preconceived notions, and previously held constructions and eschatological systems, and let only the Scripture speak for itself, perhaps it is not so inconceivable that the judgment on Jerusalem marks the beginning of God's judgment on the earth. Perhaps it is not so unbelievable that the two witnesses are resurrected and raptured when Christ comes back, just as are all believers at that time, and that this event marks the beginning of the Day of the Lord. Perhaps it is not unscriptural to understand that God's people - yes, "the Church" - will go through the time of great tribulation and that they will be allowed to suffer martyrdom, but will be protected from other elements such as the torment of the demonic beings. Perhaps this is why we have the references to the "perseverance of the Saints" right up to the time of the Harvest judgment, when God begins to pour out His wrath on the earth.

5.7 The "Perseverance of the Saints" and Harvest of Revelation Chapter 14

Here again, we have Christ coming as pictured in chapter 14, to rapture the believers and to begin to execute judgment, both happening virtually concurrently. First in that chapter we see Christ appearing on Mount Zion with the "first fruits" (the 144,000). Then we see the judgments on the followers of the beast and on Babylon the great, with the indication that there will be Saints present at the time those judgments begin, who will be persevering, and will be better off in some sense ("blessed") if they die during this time. This then is followed by the "harvest of the earth," which is presented as though there are two harvests which occur one right after the other.

This chapter would seem to be indicating two things relative to the timing of the rapture:

1) there will be Saints present when the judgments on Babylon and on the followers of the beast are about to begin;

2) there is a reaping, or rapture of the Saints that will occur before the final harvest or "grapes of wrath" judgment on the earth.

Once again, the explanation given by some would be that these are "tribulation period saints" who are being harvested here, but does not include the church. Aside from the problems discussed above with this explanation, one must wonder why so much script would be given to the rapture of the **tribulation** saints, but no explicit mention would be made in this whole book of the rapture of the church (since 11:18 is also not interpreted as including the church). This is especially curious since the first three chapters of the book are written to and about the church - yet according to PT Rapturists such as Walvoord, Pentecost, and LaHaye, there is no explicit mention of the church being raptured out anywhere in the whole book of Revelation. Of course in reality such is not the case at all.

In fact this harvest in Revelation fourteen is the harvest of all believers, including the church. It is the harvest prophesied by Joel (Joel 3:13), the ingathering of the Saints of Matthew 24:31, 1 Thessalonians 4:16-17 and 2 Thessalonians 2:1. [71] It is the time for judgment and reward for "thy bond-servants the prophets and saints" of Revelation 11:18. It is also what was promised in the 2nd and 3rd chapters of this book to those who would wake up and repent (Rev. 3:3) and overcome and persevere (Rev. 2:7, 11, 17, 25-26; 3:5, 10-12, & 21). There we see the repeated references to "the perseverance of the saints," just as we do here in 14:12 (see also 13:10).

But when men deny that every explicit description of the rapture of the church is indeed the rapture of the church, calling it instead the rapture of "tribulation saints," then they are left with no mention of the rapture of the church (how believable is that?). Instead they have to read it in to (eisegesis) passages where it really doesn't appear (such as 2 Thessalonians 2:6-7 discussed above, or Revelation 4:1, "come up here…" as per LaHaye). This is simply another example of how presuppositions combined with circular reasoning leads to what should be recognizable as glaring discrepancies. Such discrepancies however are not because of the inadequacy of Scripture to present a cogent, unambiguous, cohesive and comprehensible picture revealing a logically consistent scenario of the flow of end-time events. When allowed to speak for itself what God has revealed in this book and all the related passages of Scripture, presents a scenario in which all the pieces fit together and the relevant questions are answered without such glaring omissions and inconsistencies such as are characteristic of men's theories, no matter how prevalent or popular they may be today.

---

71 It should not be mistaken however as the harvest of Matthew 13:23-24. The passage in Matthew has irreconcilable differences and applies to the final harvest which is to occur after the Millennial reign, at the end of a Postmillennial age as discussed in a companion work, The Millennial Kingdom and The Final Judgments on Earth And the Heavenly New Jerusalem *Revisited*, Chapter 3.2 "The Final judgment in Heaven - The "*Great White Throne* judgment""

5.8 Practical Issues Related to the Various Views on the Rapture Question

Perhaps the most frequently articulated argument against the Futurists' interpretations, coming from the Historicists' and Preterists' camps, and those schools of thought that don't interpret end-time prophecy literally (especially Revelation), and especially with respect to a future rapture of the Church, is that it is such a pessimistic view. They prefer to believe that part of the Gospel is an optimistic message that the Church will prevail and be victorious even on this earth. Thus they begin with a presupposition that any prophecy to the contrary, which would be warning the Church of a time of great testing and tribulation and persecution and even judgment on this earth, can't be taken literally and must be explained away as symbolic, allegorical, or merely the hyperbolic language of poets. Rather they selectively pick out passages that tend to appear to support their preferred belief that God intends to bring about His perfect Kingdom on this earth through the Church, and will use His Saints on this earth to make that happen. Taking a very similar approach to interpreting what has happened and is currently happening in the world, they selectively pick phenomenon and events and what they see as trends, to find experiential evidence to support their views.

The same kind of approach that allows Gary DeMar[72] to insist that the prophecy about the Gog/Magog rebellion was fulfilled in the biblical account about Esther (in the book by that name), and David Chilton[73] to insist that the prophesied destruction of the whole earth was fulfilled in AD70 with the destruction of tiny Jerusalem, allows them to proclaim that the world we live in is being evangelized for Christ, and we are getting the world ready for Him to be able to assume His proper role of the sovereign ruler over a perfect kingdom.

---

72 Gary DeMar is from the school of Reformed Theology, a prominent contemporary spokesman for the Preterist school of Eschatology. He is an excellent apologist, and hosts and speaks at numerous conferences related to the subject of end-time prophecy, and the role of the church relative to government and current events. He is president of American Vision, with a website by that name (americanvision.org) and has written articles on this subject, such as "The Magog Invasion."

73 David Chilton has authored books such as one cited in this study, The Great Tribulation. He is an outspoken critic of the futurists' interpretations of end-time prophecy.

While one need not overlook the positive events and what might be current trends (albeit on a rather small scale globally speaking) that might cause us to give glory to God, it is not entirely objective or realistic to let such relatively anomalous events and trends cause us to take the ostrich approach to the far more pervasive trends and global events that seem to be leading up to a far less rosy and utopian view about our relatively near future. While Joel C. Rosenberg, an expert on Islam and Mid-Eastern affairs,[74] is optimistic about what he sees happening in the Islamic world with which he seems to be quite familiar, he remains realistic enough to know that it is not a trend that will just peacefully usher in the kingdom of God on this earth. Rather he is attacked by the DeMars of our day for seeing the path to such a victory as taking us first through the Gog/Magog prophetic event (admittedly a mistaken interpretation of Ezekiel 38-39, but certainly more biblical than DeMar's interpretation of a historic fulfillment in the story of Esther). The reality seems to be that Islam is spreading at a faster pace and making more inroads even into our Western and nominally "Christian" world, than true Christianity is accomplishing in the Islamic world. Both geo-politically and demographically, and even economically, the Mid-Eastern Islamic empire is very much on the rise as compared to the Western (including Europe and America) world that is on the decline, if not teetering on the precipice of disaster. Certainly one is hard-pressed to make the case that even the United States, let alone Europe, and certainly not Asia, is becoming more Christianized as opposed to more secularized and even antagonistic toward true Christianity. Hence, good intentions to be "optimistic" notwithstanding, the realist must realize that short of a rather major and intrusive divine intervention, the current "Church" of today, and Western Civilization as we know it, is first headed for a major conflagration and likely virtual annihilation, before any progress can be made toward establishment of any kind of a kingdom of God on this earth.

---

74 Joel Rosenberg has written a number of New York Times best-selling novels including The Last Days, The Twelfth Imam, The Ezekiel Option, The Copper Scroll, Dead Heat, The Tehran Initiative, and two nonfiction books, Epicenter, and Inside the Revolution, and he has produced two documentary films based on his nonfiction books. He is also the founder of The Joshua Fund providing humanitarian relief to Israel and her neighbors. In his documentary Inside the Revolution he writes about a spiritual revival going on in Islamic countries, an outpouring of the Holy Spirit as prophesied by Joel and Peter (in Acts 2) for the end-times. His website is joelrosenberg.com.

Hence a critical fact-based evaluation of the Preterists' optimism may not really be as optimistic as they would have us to believe.

One must seriously wonder what the Preterists and Postmillennialists of our day would have said about the major prophets, like Isaiah and Jeremiah, or even the minor prophets of the Old Testament. In fact they were physically persecuted by the "optimists" of their day, who hated the pessimism of the message those "doomsayers" were preaching. The only problem is, it was God's message they were trying to deliver, to warn the people about what was coming, and to motivate them to repent and live differently. Is the message of our modern day optimists driving us to our knees in repentance and creating in us a sense of urgency that would cause us to live differently? Not that one can notice.

Is the criterion for determining the truth of an interpretation of Scripture the question as to which interpretation is more optimistic, rejecting those that sound negative, unpleasant and pessimistic? If so those Old Testament prophets should have been rejected and silenced – as should anyone today who is interpreting Scripture literally and coming up with a somewhat negative and pessimistic message.

Even if such were the case however, then these men cited above have little of substance about which to criticize the Pretribulation Rapturists. What could be more optimistic for the Church than the message that:

"we (the Church) don't have a thing to worry about – before any of these bad things happen (which we can all see are already beginning to happen on a global scale) we will be taken out of here and won't even be affected by it." (a brief summarization of the implicit and occasionally explicit message of the PTR view)

Now that is a message that allows its adherents to see what is going on in our world without the blinders and rose-colored glasses, and see what Scripture says about where it is all heading, and not really feel the least concerned about it because it won't even really affect us who are believers, if and whenever it happens. Hence, instead of a utopian interpretation we have an "escapist" interpretation, which is probably more believable, and at the same time somewhat marketable – a welcome message, or "good news."

Unfortunately we still have a nasty problem that won't go away because we wish it to. Just as God's message through Isaiah and Jeremiah was a very **unpopular** one, a very **pessimistic** one, not a very marketable one, so is His message to the Church today. In fact, much of it is the same message only applied to us instead of only applying to ancient Israel – a message that has not yet been completely fulfilled, but probably will be in the near future. It is meant as a warning to us, the Church, as we see repeatedly stated in the introductory chapters (chapters 2-3) of the book of Revelation. It is not meant to be a message that will please us, tickle our ears (2 Timothy 4:3), and make us feel like we have nothing to be concerned about – like a happy pill to enable us to ignore what is going on in our world thinking that everything is fine, no matter what happens. Such however seems to be the effect of the PTR version – quite optimistic, but escapism that may not be reality-based, nor truly Scripture-based.

In fact, what a consistent and intellectually honest literal approach to interpreting Scripture teaches rather clearly is that this rapture is not going to happen until after "the restrainer" is taken out of the way, allowing the Antichrist to establish His global governance and set Himself up as being God (2 Thessalonians 2 couldn't be much clearer). It won't happen until God has allowed all kinds of cosmic and earthly natural disasters, and persecution and martyrdom of His Church on this earth to test and try them. This message is no more pleasing to hear, nor designed to be any more popular and marketable, than that delivered through the Old Testament prophets. It is very optimistic however, to those who are committed to trusting and obeying Christ, willing to die to self or the flesh and consider oneself dead to this world, inasmuch as it ends in Christ returning in power and glory and putting an end to the sinful evil ways of this world and its ruler, Satan. It is a day when everything will be made right, and we as Christ's followers will share in His glorification, and will begin to reign with Him in His kingdom on this earth. If this is the hope we have in mind the message is exciting and very optimistic, but realistically so.

This realistic optimism allows that we may go through some really hard times, and maybe even be allowed to give our physical lives in following our Lord, and His example. But, knowing that most of us will die anyway, this involves the promise that there will be great reward for such suffering and death. Furthermore, the literal interpretation tells us that when the worst is happening, it will only last for a short time – no more than 7 years and probably less than 3 ½ years.

However, unlike the manufactured optimism of the other interpretations and views addressed above, the implicit message of what God is perhaps "pessimistically" trying to communicate to us is that we need to be living in anticipation of this future event. It is a big deal! He isn't just telling us about these things so we can say "how nice" and then ask, "so what?" It isn't the kind of message that one can take seriously, and believe, and then just go on living as they would have anyway, the same as if they never heard the message – is it? It is a message meant to motivate us to live differently, perhaps repent of our natural complacent, self-centered, shortsighted, present-oriented, materialistic and pleasure-oriented lifestyles. It is a message that allows us to be aware of and concerned about what is going on in our world, but put it all into perspective, trusting God, knowing how it is all going to work out and that it is ultimately a very good ending. But, if we think we are supposed to be gone (raptured out) before all hell breaks loose, and before the global ruler requires us to sign up for his world-wide economic program to survive, how will we understand what is going on when it actually happens, and put it all in proper perspective? At best, a lot of disillusionment and doubts and fears will be issues, and it seems very likely that many will lose their faith, certainly their optimism.

5.9 A Summary View

Perhaps the simplest explanation of what unfolds in Revelation is the best:

a. The **Day of the Lord** begins when the last (seventh) *trumpet* sounds, at which time **the resurrection and rapture occurs** (the one and only "rapture"), including the resurrection and rapture of the two Witnesses. Those who are raptured are the church. They are those who have survived the martyrdom and persevered through the time of Great Tribulation, and have not received the mark of the Beast, nor worshipped him.

b. The **Day of the Lord** marks the beginning of God's judgment on the earth, which begins with the earthquake in Jerusalem, as Christ returns to earth with His army, and personally takes the lead in the battle against the Great Dragon, the Beast, and all the followers of the Beast.

c. The **Day of the Lord** includes the battle of HarMagedon, at which time the Kings of the Earth with what may be a 200 million man army[75] are defeated in a huge blood bath. It also includes the **ultimate final** judgment of Babylon the Great, the beginning of which judgment – the fall of Babylon - apparently precedes the battle of HarMagedon.

d. **The Day of the Lord** consummates with the great earthquakes and thunder and lightening and hailstorm, at which time the earth as we know it is destroyed by burning, and the "heavens will pass away" (2 Pet. 3:10 & 12). This will not be a total annihilation of the heavens and earth, but a total destruction leading to a renovation resulting in the "new heavens and a new earth," [76] to make this earth habitable again for Christ's millennial reign.

---

75 If we take the 200 million as a literal army of horsemen, though as discussed in a companion work, The Seals, Trumpets, and Bowls of Revelation Revisited, that may not be the best interpretation of as it may be figurative language describing the effects of the cosmic event of comet strikes. In any case the Battle of HarMagedon will involve an unprecedented army of horsemen which will be destroyed at that time.

76 Given that the Millennial reign of Christ is to occur on this earth, some would argue that 2 Peter 3:10 & 12 must be another final judgment which occurs after the Millennium, identifying it with the judgment on Gog/Magog of Revelation 20:7-10. They thus interpret those passages as describing a complete annihilation of the present heavens and earth, and the beginning of the eternal state that we usually call heaven. However, there are several problems with this understanding of the 2 Peter passage, which they cannot adequately explain. First, if God does not recreate supernaturally a renewed heaven and earth, as 2 Peter says, before Christ begins His millennial reign on this earth (as Isaiah tells us so clearly in Isaiah 65:17), what kind of a mess does He have, and how will it be an environment that anyone would ever want to live in after the massive destruction and pollution caused by the cosmic disturbances, and the *trumpet* and *bowl* judgments? Second, the *"thief in the night"* warning found in that passage in 2nd Peter could only apply to the return of Christ at the *"day of the Lord"* advent, since everyone will know exactly when the close of the 1000 years will be occurring, and it will certainly not be coming *"as a thief in the night."* The explanation that this *"day of the Lord"* is the whole period of 1007 years extending from a pre-tribulation rapture to the post-millennial judgment on God-Magog, is a nonsensical forced interpretation designed to allow this passage to accommodate the PTR theory. Ironically, some such as Dr. Pentecost (see p 174 of Things to Come) then use this passage in 2 Peter to support that same interpretation of the *"day of the Lord"* (the very passage such an interpretation is designed to accommodate) – a perfect example of circular reasoning.

e. The time that lapses from the beginning of this "day of the Lord" when Christ returns, until the judgments on the earth is finished, and the millennial temple is built and cleansed, and the millennial priests are purified and the situation as described in Ezekiel 40-46 is initially implemented, may be the 75 day extension prophesied by Daniel ("1335 days" after the "abomination of desolation is set up" (Dan. 12:11-12)).

CHAPTER 6

SUMMARY AND CONCLUSIONS

The purpose of this study, as the title suggests, is primarily to evaluate the currently popular Pretribulation Rapture view and the Dispensationalist approach to interpreting prophetic Scripture that inspires it. In the process we begin with a look at the underlying assumptions and presuppositions that drive those interpretations and conclusions. This must begin with the basic approach to interpreting Scripture, and prophetic passages in particular, comparing the more allegorical approaches (the language of prophecy is symbolic, poetic and hyperbolic - not to be taken literally) of the Historicists, Preterits, Postmillennialists and Idealists with the more literal approaches of the Futurists. The argument is made that the only approach which makes any sense after all, and can claim any degree of objectivity and consistency and testability with respect to corroborating evidence, is the literal approach and the ensuing Futurists interpretations of Bible prophecy.

However, even in the literalist and futurist camp there are varying degrees of literalness, and intellectual integrity with respect to compliance with objective rules of interpretation and exegesis and reason or logic. Specifically the currently popular school of Dispensational Theology and the associated Pretribulation Rapture view are evaluated with respect to the accuracy of their interpretations of Scripture, and their conformance to the rules of logic and reason. The conclusion is that while they are an improvement over the non-literal approaches of the Idealists, Historicists, Preterits, and Postmillennialists, they are nonetheless found wanting in many respects, such that their theories and scenarios appear to be neither entirely scriptural nor rational.

This conclusion is supported by the evidence derived from analysis of such basic tenets and key interpretations and concepts as:

- the Dispensational Hermeneutic;
- the presupposition of a Pretribulation Rapture which is not articulated anywhere in Scripture;
- the forced and unscriptural interpretation of "the day of the Lord," and "the day of wrath";
- the convoluted and self-contradictory "imminence" doctrine;
- the inattention to such details as "the last trump;"
- the failure to recognize the pattern of revelation in the book of Revelation;
- the failure to accept the clear articulation of Scripture with respect to the timing of the destruction of the present heaven and earth, the creation of the new heaven and earth.

However, the purpose of this research and analysis is not primarily to critique and find fault with a popular perhaps mainstream view among conservative evangelicals, but to try to determine what God is trying to communicate to us about what is going to happen in those end-times. It involved an attempt to become aware of, and to critically evaluate my own personal presuppositions and biases - which were originally the products of indoctrination in this very same Dispensationalist Pretribulation Rapture school of Theology and Eschatologically. It is an attempt to let Scripture speak for itself, applying the rules of hermeneutics (the objective rules) and honest exegesis, and the rules of logic and reason, as objectively as possible. And it is a venture of faith, trusting God to keep His promise to enlighten and guide my understanding as I depend upon Him to show me what He is trying to communicate. The assumption was that as a result of the right process and dependence on God rather than on men, a picture would unfold and a scenario would emerge that would be completely logical, and consistent with identifiable realities, since it would only be a description of reality. But even more importantly, it would be a scenario which would be consistent with all the Scripture that can be brought to bear on every aspect of the scenario, without forcing interpretations, manipulating words, ignoring some passages while selectively cherry picking others that fit a preconceived theory or scenario or presuppositions.

What has emerged is an amazing testimony to the supernatural nature of the inspired Word of God as Divine revelation. God's word is complete and completely consistent and coherent without contradictions or holes in the logic. While the scenario that emerged clearly involves a sovereign God in control with timely interventions of a supernatural nature, it also involves processes and phenomena of nature, as well as geo-political developments, the descriptions of which are consistent with known science and history and current events. It is a scenario that is not only believable, but demonstrably scriptural as well, as born out by the pervasive use of citations and quotes from Scripture to document every point that is made throughout.[77]

The following briefly summarizes this scenario and the interpretations that are the results of this study and research, which is perhaps best labeled as a **Posttribulation Prewrath Rapture View** (see figure 6.-1). In this proposed view:

- The church is very much present on earth during the Tribulation Period and is in fact being purified and tested and persecuted by Satan and his followers;
- The first six seals, and the first six trumpets and bowls are events of nature and the works of Satan, the Beast and their followers - not the wrath of God;
- The seals, trumpets and bowls are more parallel than sequential, albeit progressive;
- The sixth seal is the much prophesied sign event, a catastrophic cosmic event or series of events that ultimately destroys the earth;
- The consummation of the sixth seal, seventh trumpet and seventh bowl coincide with the Battle of HarMageddon which is when the wrath of God is poured out - the "day of wrath;"
- The "Day of the Lord" is "the day of wrath" which is in fact a brief period of time in which God judges the earth exactly as

---

[77] Indeed it is hoped that one of the criticisms of this work will be that if anything too much Scripture is used too often for the readers taste.

described repeatedly throughout Scripture, especially in 2 Peter 3, and Revelation 19;

- It is the "second coming of Christ," the long awaited "parousia";
- it is when He raises from the dead all those who are saved, and rescues those still alive on earth who are His followers as the church is raptured out;
- In heaven there is the "marriage of the Lamb" (or "marriage supper of the Lamb") and the "judgment Seat of Christ " ("Bema") which is the judgment in heaven of all the saved; these receive their reward for their works, and enter their eternal home in heaven;
- Christ returns to earth with His host (including the raptured and resurrected Saints) for the Battle of Harmageddon in which He defeats all His foes;
- Then comes the outpouring of God's wrath on the earth and its inhabitants;
- At that time God destroys the heaven and earth as we know them (though not total annihilation);
- At that time the Beast and the False Prophet are sent to Hell, their followers are killed, and Satan is imprisoned for a thousand year sentence;
- After judging the earth and its inhabitants - a complete destruction, He then creates the new heaven and earth;
- He then sets up His Millennial kingdom, which is also an eternal kingdom;
- This is a thousand year era in which men's hearts are changed, righteousness and peace reign, and sin is not present, though men on earth who are still mortals, still die from old age and children are born;
- After that thousand year reign of Christ on earth, there is a resurrection of the rest of the dead - i.e. the unsaved dead and those who die during the Millennium and Satan is released from his prison;
- During that Postmillennial period the gospel is preached throughout the world to those who had never heard, by the surviving and resurrected Millenarians, and many are saved;

- But Satan uses Gog of Magog to organize all those who reject the Gospel to form a huge army, which marches on Jerusalem;
- Then God intervenes and destroys Gog and all of his followers;
- He also judges all those who were not part of the first resurrection and judgment (i.e. those Saints who are already in heaven) at the Great White Throne judgment, and casts all those into Hell whose names are not found written in the book of life.
- Those on earth who are in the book of life, who have survived the Millennial reign on earth, and the Post-Millennial era (i.e. were those of the second resurrection who repent and accept Christ), continue in His earthly kingdom for eternity;
- The New Jerusalem of Revelation is the eternal heavenly home of all those saved believers who were rapture/resurrected at the second coming of Christ;
- The New Jerusalem of Ezekiel 40-48 is the earthly Kingdom of God which begins in the Millennium and continues through the Postmillennium into the Eternal State;
- It is the eternal home of all those saved who were not part of the first resurrection, Millennial Saints and converts during the Postmillennial worldwide evangelism, whose names were written in the Lamb's Book of Life;
- The judgment of the Gog rebellion during the Postmillennium is the last judgment on earth after which the Kingdom of God on earth is finally purged and cleansed forever;
- The Great White throne judgment coincides with the last earthly judgment and the fate of all those not in the Book of Life, including Satan, is determined, which is eternity in Hell.[78]

---

78 Several of these points are not addressed in this book, such as the Seals, Trumpets and Bowls, the Millennial Kingdom and the New Jerusalem, the Postmillennial era and the Gog/Magog rebellion, and the Final Judgments on earth, but are the subjects of other books by this author, including The Seals, Trumpets and Bowls of Revelation Revisited, Gog/Magog Revisited, and The Millennial Kingdom and The Final Judgments on Earth And the Heavenly New Jerusalem *Revisited.*

Day of the Lord	Millennium	Post Millennium	Eternal State
Christ returns 1st resurrection and Rapture	Church in heavenly New Jerusalem	Heaven – New Jerusalem Christ reigns - Eternal Kingdom of God on Earth continues	
Marriage Supper of the Lamb	Satan imprisoned	Satan released Resurrection of rest of the rest of the dead	
Judgment Seat of Christ – rewards give to Saints	Resurrected Saints reign with Christ	Gog/Magog rebellion Jerusalem attacked	
Conquers foes Destroys the earth	Complete obedience and Righteousness - Lion lies with the lamb	God intervenes - Final judgment on earth Great White Throne judgment	Satan and unsaved condemned to Hell for eternity
Creates new heaven & earth	Perfect Edenic environment	All Israel saved – complete restoration and regeneration Gospel preached to the whole world – many Gentiles saved	No more physical death
	Children are born		
	People live 100+ years		
	People die physically		
	Millennial Temple Worship	Priesthood purified - Temple worship on earth continues	

Postribulation Prewrath Rapture View Figure 6.-1

With this last chapter of the last book of the Bible divine revelation ends, as does the whole story of human history - or is it just the beginning?

BIBLIOGRAPHY

[1] Alford, Henry. <u>New Testament for English Readers</u>, Vol. 4, "The Revelation of John," Baker Book House, Grand Rapids MI 49506, 1983.

[2] Arndt, William F. & Gingrich, F. Wilbur. <u>A Greek-English Lexicon of the New Testament and Other Early Christian Literature. 2nd edition from Walter Bauer's fifth edition 1958.</u> The University of Chicago Press, Chicago and London.

[3] Baxter, J. Sidlow. <u>Explore the Book</u>, Zondervan Publishing House, Grand Rapids, MI 49506. 1960.

[4] Chafer, L.S. revised by Walvoord, J.F. <u>Major Bible Themes</u>, Zondervan Publishing House, Grand Rapids, MI 49506, 1974.

[5] Chambers, W. & R. <u>Chamber's Encyclopedia</u>, Vol. II, Collier Publisher, New York, 1888.

[6] Chamberlain, William Douglas. <u>An Exegetical Grammar of the Greek New Testament.</u> Baker Book House, Grand Rapids, Michigan, 1941.

[7] Chilton, David. <u>The Great Tribulation</u>, Dominion Press, Tyler TX 75711, 1987.

[8] Constable, Thomas. "1 Thessalonians," <u>The Bible Knowledge Commentary, New Testament Edition</u>. Victor Books, SP Publications, Inc., Wheaton IL 60187. 1983.

[9] Dyer, Charles H. <u>World News and Bible Prophecy</u>. Tyndale House Publishers, Wheaton IL, 1993.

[10] endtimes.org/dispens.html

[11] Eusebius. The History of the Church from Christ to Constantine, Book 5, 8.9; as translated by G. A. Williamson. Penguin Books, Dorset Press, 1965.

[12] Gentry, Kenneth L. Jr. Postmillennialism Made Easy, Apologetic Group Media, Draper, VA., 2009.

[13] Hartill, J. Edwin. Principles of Biblical Hermeneutics. Zondervan Publishing House, Grand Rapids MI 49506. 1947.

[14] Historicism Research Foundation, www.historicism.net.

[15] Ironside, H. A. Lectures on Daniel the Prophet. 2nd ed. Loizeaux Brothers, New Jersey. 1920.

[16] Jeffrey, Grant R. Apocalypse The Coming Judgment of the Nations. Bantam Books. 1994.

[17] Keil, C.F. & F. Delitzsch. Keil & Delitzsch Commentary on the Old Testament Vol. 5: Psalms, Electronic Edition STEP Files Copyright © 2005, QuickVerse.

[18] LaHaye, Tim. Revelation Unveiled, Zondervan, Grand Rapids, Michigan, 49530, 1999 (paperback edition).

[19] LaHaye, Tim and Hindson, Ed. General Editors. The Popular Encyclopedia of Bible Prophecy, Harvest House Publishers, Eugene Oregon, 97402, 2004.

[20] LaHaye, Tim and Ice, Thomas. Charting The End Times, Harvest House Publishers, Eugene Oregon 97402, 2001.

[21] Levy, David M. Revelation – Hearing the Last Word. The Friends of the Gospel Ministry Inc., Bellmar NJ08099, 1999.

[22] Levitt, Zola. Dateline Jerusalem – News and Views from the World's Flashpoint of Bible Prophecy. Balfour Books, Green Forest, AR 7638, 2005.

[23] Marshall, Alfred. NASB-NIV Parallel New Testament in Greek and English; from the 21st edition of Eberhard Nestle's *Novum Testamentum Graece)*. Regency Reference Library, Zondervan Publishing House, Grand Rapids, MI 49506,1987.

[24] Morris, Cannon Leon. The Revelation of St. John. The Tyndale New Testament Commentaries; ed. By R.V.G. Tasker, M.A., D.D. Eerdman's Publishing Co., Grand Rapids, MI; Tyndale Press, 1981.

[25] Microsoft Encarta 98 Encyclopedia.

[26] Moulton, H.K. The Analytical Greek Lexicon Revised . 1978 edition. Zondervan Publishing House, Grand Rapids, MI 49506.

[27] Open Bible Expanded Edition (Thomas Nelson Publishers, 1985)

[28] Pentecost, J. Dwight. Things to Come. Zondervan Publishing House, Grand Rapids MI 49506. 1958.

[29] Richardson, Joel. The Islamic Antichrist, WND (World NetDaily) Books, Los Angeles, CA, 2009.

[30] Robertson, Archibald Thomas. Word Pictures in the New Testament. Broadman Press, Nashville TN, 1933.

[31] Rosenthal, Marvin J. The Pre-wrath Rapture of the Church. Thomas Nelson Publishers, Nashville TN. 1990.

[32] Russell, J. Stuart. The Parousia: A Critical Inquiry into the New Testament Doctrine of Our Lord's Second Coming. London: Daldy, Isbister, 1878.

[33] Scofield, C. I. The New Scofield Reference Bible, Oxford University Press, Inc., NY, 1967.

[34] Seiss, Joseph A. The Apocalypse - Exposition of the Book of Revelation. Kregel Publications, Grand Rapids, MI 49501. 1987 reprint of original 1900 by C.C. Cook.

[35] Shoebat, Walid, and Richardson, Joel. God's War on Terror - Islam, Prophecy and the Bible; Top Executive Media, 2010.

[36] Simons, Geoff. Iraq – From Sumer to Saddam, 2nd ed. St. Martin's Press, New York NY, 1996.

[37] Snell, H. H. Notes on the Revelation, W. H. Broom, 1878.

[38] Sookhdeo, Patrick. Global Jihad - The Future in the Face of Militant Islam, Isaac Publishing, 6729 Curran St., McLean VA 22101, second printing, Nov. 2007.

[39] Sproul, R. C. The Last Days According to Jesus. Baker Books, Grand Rapids, MI, 1998, fourth printing June 2003.

[40] Summers, Ray. Essentials of New Testament Greek, Broadman Press, Nashville Tennessee, 1950.

[41] Thayer, Joseph Henry. A Greek-English Lexicon of the New Testament. Mott Media, Milford, MI, 1977.

[42] Van Kampen, Robert. The Sign of Christ's Coming and the End of the Age. Crossway Books, Wheaton IL. 1992.

[43] Van Ryn, August. Notes on the Book of Revelation. Walterick Publishers, Kansas City, KA. 1960.

[44] Walvoord, John F. "Revelation", The Bible Knowledge Commentary, New Testament Edition. Victor Books, SP Publications, Inc., Wheaton IL 60187. 1983.

[45] --------------; Armageddon, Oil and the Middle East Crisis. Zondervan Publishing House, Grand Rapids MI 49506, 1990.

[46] --------------; Daniel – The Key to Prophetic Revelation. Moody Press, Chicago, 1971.

[47] --------------; The Revelation of Jesus Christ. Moody Press, Chicago, 1966.

[48] Wigram, George, V. The Englishman's Greek Concordance of the New Testament. Baker Book House, Grand Rapids, MI 1979.

[49] Webster, Noah & McKechine, Jean L. Webster' New Universal Unabridged Dictionary, 2nd Ed., Simon & Schuster, New York, NY 10020, 1983.

[50] Zondervan NIV Bible Commentary